Organizational Implementation
The Design in Use of Information Systems

Synthesis Lectures on Human-Centered Informatics

Editor
John M. Carroll, *Penn State University*

Human-Centered Informatics (HCI) is the intersection of the cultural, the social, the cognitive, and the aesthetic with computing and information technology. It encompasses a huge range of issues, theories, technologies, designs, tools, environments, and human experiences in knowledge work, recreation and leisure activity, teaching and learning, and the potpourri of everyday life. The series publishes state-of-the-art syntheses, case studies, and tutorials in key areas. It shares the focus of leading international conferences in HCI.

Organizational Implementation: The Design in Use of Information Systems
Morten Hertzum

Data-Driven Personas
Bernard J. Jansen, Joni Salminen, Soon-gyo Jung, and Kathleen Guan

Worth-Focused Design, Book 2: Approaches, Context, and Case Studies
Gilbert Cockton

Worth-Focused Design, Book 1: Balance, Integration, and Generosity
Gilbert Cockton

Statistics for HCI: Making Sense of Quantitative Datas
Alan Dix

Usabiity Testing: A Practitioner's Guide to Evaluating the User Experience
Morten Hertzum

Geographical Design: Spatial Cognition and Geographical Information Science, Second Edition
Stephen C. Hirtle

Human-Computer Interactions in Museums
Eva Hornecker and Luigina Ciolfi

Encounters with HCI Pioneers: A Personal History and Photo Journal
Ben Shneiderman

Organizational Implementation: The Design in Use of Information Systems
Morten Hertzum

ISBN: 978-3-031-01104-7   print
ISBN: 978-3-031-02232-6   ebook
ISBN: 978-3-031-00212-0   hardcover

DOI 10.1007/978-3-031-02232-6

A Publication in the Springer series
SYNTHESIS LECTURES ON HUMAN-CENTERED INFORMATICS
Lecture #49

Series Editor: John M. Carroll, Penn State University

Series ISSN   1946-7680   Print   1946-7699   Electronic

Organizational Implementation

The Design in Use of Information Systems

Morten Hertzum
University of Copenhagen, Copenhagen, Denmark

SYNTHESIS LECTURES ON HUMAN-CENTERED INFORMATICS #49

ABSTRACT

Information systems are part and parcel of organizations. Yet, organizations often struggle to realize the benefits that motivate their introduction of these systems. To derive benefit from a new information system, it must be integrated into the structures and processes of the organization. That is, the system must be organizationally implemented. This book is about organizational implementation, which requires thorough preparations but also continues long after the system has gone live: (1) During the preparations, the implementation is planned. This phase includes specifying the effects pursued with the system, adapting the system and organization to each other, and obtaining buy-in for the planned change. (2) At go-live, the system is put to operational use and the associated organizational changes take effect. This phase is about insisting on the planned change even though go-live is normally hectic and accompanied by a productivity dip. (3) During continued use after go-live, implementation continues as design in use. This phase is long and improvisational. It includes following up on effects realization, but it is just as much about embracing the opportunities that emerge from using the system. Apart from covering the three phases of organizational implementation, the book inserts implementation in an organizational-change context and discusses barriers to implementation as well as boosters of implementation. The book concludes with an outlook to larger-scale issues beyond the implementation of one system in one organization and with an overview of the competences needed in the implementation team, which runs the organizational implementation.

KEYWORDS

benefits realization, design in use, effects specification, go-live, human–computer interaction, implementation team, organizational implementation, organizational change, sociotechnical change, system adoption, system configuration, tailoring, technology acceptance

Contents

Acknowledgments

I have been interested in the organizational implementation of information systems since the early 1990s. At that time, paper was still the technology of choice in many organizations and more computers were standalone than networked. Technology, organizations, and society have changed substantially since then, but organizational implementation has remained nontrivial. This book has grown out of my research on the topic over the last three decades. Most of this research has been conducted in collaboration with colleagues who have contributed invaluably, and in various ways, to my thinking about organizational implementation. Without their contributions, I would not have been in a position to write this book. I am particularly indebted to Margunn Aanestad, Jose Abdelnour-Nocera, Alexandre Alapetite, Henning Boje Andersen, Jørgen Bansler, Anders Barlach, Jesper Berger, Pernille Bjørn, Keld Bødker, Torkil Clemmensen, Gunnar Ellingsen, Benedicte Fleron, Erik Frøkjær, Maren Sander Granlien, Erling Havn, Helena Karasti, Maria Ie Manikas, Troels Mønsted, Rasmus Rasmussen, Michel Sassene, Jesper Simonsen, Dineshkumar Singh, Veerendra Veer Singh, and Arnvør á Torkilsheyggi. In addition, I wish to extend my thanks to the many practitioners who, in spite of their busy schedules, have been prepared to take part in our empirical studies.

CHAPTER 1

Introduction

Information systems have transformed organizations and continue to do so. Brick-and-mortar banks have given way to e-banking and online payments (Chen et al., 2017). Libraries are turning toward communal and cultural activities because citizens increasingly find information online (Leorke et al., 2018). Sports organizations have started to embrace e-sport, which introduces an entirely new line of professional athletes (Heere, 2018). Workplaces have become more distributed because information technology (IT) provides possibilities for communicating and collaborating across distance (Olson and Olson, 2014). The paper trail associated with organizational proceedings has increasingly become electronic (Mosweu and Mosweu, 2018). It has become big business to mine the electronic footprints of our activities (Inanc-Demir and Kozak, 2019).

At the same time, organizations often struggle to realize the benefits that motivate their introduction of new information systems (Fitzgerald et al., 2014; Markus, 2004; Standish Group, 2020). Some systems are used for only a subset of the activities they were intended to support (Granlien and Hertzum, 2012). Others fail altogether because they are rejected by a powerful user group (Bhattacherjee et al., 2013). Still others succeed in one organization but fail in another (Aarts and Berg, 2006). The Standish Group publishes a biannual report with data about the success rate of IT projects. If success is defined as on time, on budget, and with a satisfactory result, then 31% of projects are successful, 50% are challenged, and 19% are failures (Standish Group, 2020).

1.1 ORGANIZATIONAL IMPLEMENTATION

While some systems fail because they are technically flawed, there are also many technically sound systems that are challenged or fail for organizational reasons. This book is about the implementation of information systems in organizational settings. When an organization adopts an information system, it must be integrated into the structures and processes of the organization. That is, the organization must adapt to the system, which in its turn must be adapted to the organization (Leonard-Barton, 1988). This mutual adaptation involves work-practice changes, system configurations, and the gradual realization of which affordances the system has—and lacks—in relation to the work performed in the organization. In brief, *organizational implementation* is:

> the process of integrating a technological system into the structures and processes of
> an organization to accomplish desired change.

This definition covers off-the-shelf and custom-made systems, it avoids restricting implementation to the early use of a system, and it links implementation to organizational change. The starting point of organizational implementation is the managerial decision to adopt the system. Because this decision has been made before organizational implementation starts, the system vendor has already been selected and the system specified. However, the development of the system has not necessarily been finalized when the preparations for its organizational implementation start. Specifically, the system and organization have not yet been configured for each other. The responsibility for integrating the system into the organization typically rests with an implementation team established by management (Metz and Bartley, 2020). To succeed, this team needs to involve the organization in the implementation process.

The system may be for intra-departmental, organization-wide, or inter-organizational use. With larger scale, complexity increases. More users must be trained, more procedures revised, more data migrated, more interdependencies realigned, and so forth. Yet even for an intra-departmental system, the implementation team must cover a diverse mix of competences. To cover all the needed competences, implementation teams are dependent on collaboration with other actors. A steering committee will oversee the work of the implementation team and grant it authority to change the organization. External consultants, often employed by the system vendor, can supply technical competence about the system and how to configure it. Furthermore, champions, super users, and tinkerers are key contributors to the organizational implementation. Figure 1.1 gives an overview of the actors who surround the implementation team.

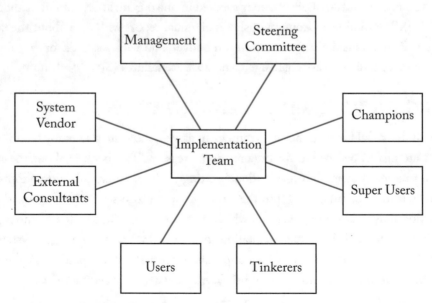

Figure 1.1: The implementation team and its collaborators.

Many troubled information systems result from a poor fit between the system and the organization (Howard and Rose, 2019; Zigurs and Buckland, 1998). Organizational implementation aims to find solutions to such troubles, which are often not realized, at least not fully, until the users start using the system for real work. Relatedly, many successful information systems result, at least partly, from implementation efforts to exploit opportunities that did not emerge until the users started using the system for real work. The successful implementation process requires adaptation, integration, and creative solutions to emergent issues. It is the continuation of design into use, rather than the transition from design to use.

1.2   SYSTEM VIEW ON ORGANIZATIONAL IMPLEMENTATION

For the managers and developers who decide and develop an information system, the system is the prime focus of attention and organizational implementation is a phase in the system life-cycle. Figure 1.2 illustrates this system-centric view of organizational implementation. The process starts with chartering, which is the phase during which the vision about a new system is proposed, approved, and funded (Markus, 2004). Chartering results in a business case that describes how the new system will make work more productive, satisfying, or both. After chartering, the development of the system takes place. It is the phase during which requirements are specified in detail, the information system is acquired or built, and the associated changes in organizational structures and processes are planned. At go-live, the system enters into operational use. Within the system view on organizational implementation, go-live also marks the transition from technical development to organizational implementation.

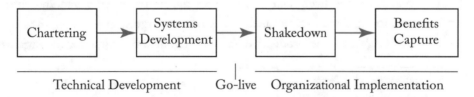

Figure 1.2: System view on organizational implementation, based on Markus (2004).

While organizational implementation must be prepared before go-live, it happens from go-live onward. The phase immediately after go-live is shakedown, during which the organization starts using the system and operating according to the changed procedures. This phase is about troubleshooting and reaching the state of routine use. Ideally, shakedown is brief and followed by a long phase of benefits capture. During benefits capture, the organization profits from the system and the new ways of working. This phase is characterized by routine use but may also involve upgrades and other improvement efforts.

The system view makes shakedown the critical part of organizational implementation. It may even be tempting to equate organizational implementation with shakedown. That would, however, be an oversimplification because it would tend to grant primacy to the system at the expense of the local practices in the organization. Shakedown harbors a belief that the system is right and, thereby, that the best way forward is to implement the system as planned. This belief under-recognizes how important the numerous, interrelated local practices are to a well-functioning organization and, thereby, to the successful implementation of an information system. It takes time for new practices to form. They emerge over an extended period of time and reinforce, revise, and reject different parts of the planned change (Orlikowski, 1996). That is, they influence benefits capture.

1.3   PRACTICE VIEW ON ORGANIZATIONAL IMPLEMENTATION

The practice view on organizational implementation stands in contrast to the system view. According to the practice view, the daily work—the practice—has primacy for those working in an organization (Feldman and Orlikowski, 2011; Miettinen et al., 2009). Performing the daily work involves an often complex configuration of people, systems, tasks, and structures. This configuration has been established over time, creates a negotiated order, and thereby aligns collaborative activities. While information systems are a means to support the daily work, their organizational implementation consumes resources that would otherwise be available for getting today's work done. Figure 1.3 illustrates how the people in an organization divide their attention and resources between using the present work configuration to get their work done and redesigning the work configuration to become able to work more effectively and efficiently in the future. It often requires most, if not all, of the staff's attention and resources to meet work-output targets. In addition, the hours spent meeting work-output targets are the productive hours that generate income for the organization.

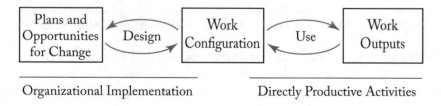

Figure 1.3: Practice view on organizational implementation.

An organization that adopts an information system cannot bill the implementation activities to its clients. The organization undertakes these activities for its own sake, for example to become more competitive in future bids for contracts. The implementation activities require a focus on how the work can be done differently, rather than on getting it done here and now. Many employees are primarily concerned with getting their work done and perceive the activities of organizational implementation as secondary (Hertzum and Torkilsheyggi, 2019). After all, most nurses care more about patients than information systems. Similarly, most accountants, biochemists, curators, dentists, engineers, and so forth care more about their professional specialty than about information systems. These employees have little patience with information systems and may lose faith in a hard-to-learn system before they have worked through shakedown.

Some employees have a keen interest in devising improved ways of working. These innovators and tinkerers are important because they have visions for the use of information systems. However, their concern for the long-term evolution of their organization means that they tend to have a more open-ended time perspective than IT project staff, who work within project deadlines (Karasti et al., 2010). This difference in time perspective creates one pressure for completing the implementation project within the deadline set for shakedown and another for a series of implementation efforts spaced over the effective lifetime of the system. While the former aligns with the system view, the latter caters for exploiting emergent uses of the system to improve organizational practices. To accomplish their task, the implementation team needs to balance the system and practice views.

1.4   CHAPTER OUTLINE

The remaining chapters of this book describe and discuss organizational implementation from the position that it is equally about system and practice. Disregarding either view would make organizational implementation difficult to accomplish. To merge the system and practice views, organizational implementation is treated as design in use. If you are only interested in guidance on conducting organizational implementation, you can skip directly to Chapters 4–7. They are the main chapters of the book. Chapters 2 and 3 provide background about organizational change and technology adoption. Chapter 8 concludes the book.

We start with the context and rationale for implementing information systems. Chapter 2, "The Context and Rationale: Organizational Change," will position the implementation of information systems in the larger activity of organizational change. Organizations adopt information systems to bring about desired change, but the organizational response to systems after go-live also reshapes which changes are seen as possible and desirable. This chapter elaborates organizational change by discussing its sociotechnical nature, its temporality, its depth, and organizations' readiness for it.

Chapter 3, "Technology Adoption: Boosters and Barriers," will explore the reasons for success, trouble, and failure in organizational implementation. These reasons are mostly about the fit between the technology and the organization. Management makes the decision to adopt a system on the basis of its positive assessment of this fit. The users form their perception of the fit when they experience the system. For both management and users, adoption results from interactions among factors that boost adoption and barriers that thwart it. This chapter covers the two-stage adoption process, boosters of adoption, and barriers to adoption.

Chapter 4, "Implementing Information Systems: Three Phases," will clarify that organizational implementation is a design-in-use process. That is, design does not stop at go-live but continues during use. Both before and after go-live, this design process involves the mutual adaptation of organization and technology. This chapter outlines the three phases of organizational implementation, to be elaborated in the following chapters.

Chapter 5, "Preparations: Planning the Implementation," will elaborate the phase that precedes go-live. This phase includes effects specification, system configuration, new procedures, user training, and realigning incentives. The mutual adaptation of system and organization creates both opportunities and challenges. On the one hand, the preparations can influence the finalization of the system. On the other hand, activities such as user training are dependent on access to the final system. This chapter also covers standardization, user participation, pilot implementation, and champions.

Chapter 6, "Going Live: The Initial, Planned Change," will cover the phase during which the system enters into operational use and the associated organizational changes take effect. It is at this point that the consequences of the system become salient to its users. Many users experience go-live as hectic and uncertain. To keep it brief, some organizations take a big-bang approach; others opt for incremental implementation. This chapter is about the implementation approach, data migration, precautions against errors, super users, and the productivity dip that accompanies go-live.

Chapter 7, "Continuing Design During Use: The Long, Improvisational Process," will elaborate the continuation of and support for organizational implementation during operational use. This phase includes following up on the realization of the planned effects, but it is just as much about embracing the further opportunities that emerge from using the system. Often, these opportunities initially emerge as workarounds devised by innovative users, who tinker with the system. This chapter covers effects follow-up, workarounds, tinkerers, and continual implementation support.

Chapter 8, "The Larger Picture and the Local Needs," will conclude the book by providing an outlook to two issues beyond the implementation of one system in one place. First, systems with infrastructural properties have a scale and scope that magnify the complexities of organizational implementation. Second, system vendors involve their client communities in generification activities, which determine how the systems can subsequently be configured for individual clients. These larger-scale issues complement how organizational implementation is perceived and performed locally. The chapter ends by cataloging the competences needed locally in the implementation team.

This book is intended for current and prospective members of implementation teams. It may also be useful for others with an interest in understanding organizational implementation. This audience forms a mixed group of practitioners, students, and researchers. The practitioners may be IT developers involved in preparing, supporting, and following up on go-live, or they may be local staff, including super users, with the responsibility for IT implementation and support. The students and researchers may be from technical fields and mainly have a system view on organizational implementation, or they may be from organizational fields and have more of a practice view. Depending on background, some parts of the book will refresh familiar material, while other parts will introduce new issues and perspectives. I hope the book will serve as a common framework for people who approach organizational implementation from different backgrounds.

CHAPTER 2

The Context and Rationale: Organizational Change

Information systems are a means to an end. Organizations adopt them to bring about desired change. In this sense, organizational change is the rationale for implementing information systems, and implementation success is about accomplishing the desired change. At the same time, the organizational response to an information system after go-live gradually reshapes what changes the organization sees as possible and desirable. This response depends on the system as well as on how the organization deals with change. That is, organizational change is also the context—not only the rationale—for implementing information systems.

This chapter starts by positioning the implementation of information systems in the larger activity of organizational change (Section 2.1). While change is necessary for organizations to remain effective and competitive, it is not easy to accomplish. To appreciate the complexity, three aspects of organizational change will be elaborated: temporality, depth, and readiness. Temporality is discussed in terms of the distinction between episodic and continuous change (Section 2.2), depth in terms of the distinction between single-loop and double-loop learning (Section 2.3), and readiness in terms the distinction between bureaucratic and organic organizations (Section 2.4). These discussions serve to contextualize organizational implementation.

2.1   ORGANIZATIONAL CHANGE IS SOCIOTECHNICAL

Organizations change through changes in their component parts. Leavitt (1965) defines organizations as consisting of four interdependent components; see Figure 2.1. The *people* working in an organization include management, operational staff, and support staff. Different people have different competences, for example acquired through formal education or on-the-job training, and they perform different tasks. Each *task* contributes to the production of the goods or services supplied by the organization. The tasks require common or specialist competences, are part of line or staff functions, and involve the use of information systems or other technologies. *Technology* is the machinery and equipment used by the people in performing their tasks. While the use of some technologies is mandated by the organization, the use of others is left to the discretion of individual people or teams. Finally, *structure* refers to the lines of communication, norms of performance, system of authority, and division of labor. The structure ties tasks together in a complete production process and stipulates who performs which tasks.

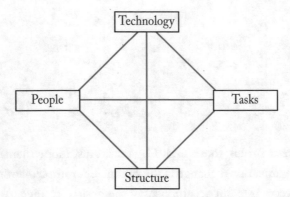

Figure 2.1: Organizations change through changes in four interdependent components, based on Leavitt (1965).

The crucial insight from Figure 2.1 is not its four components as such, but their interdependence. The interdependence has profound consequences for organizational change: "Clearly, most efforts to effect change, whether they begin with people, technology, structure, or task, soon must deal with the others" (Leavitt, 1965, p. 1145).

Efforts restricted to a single component have limited potential to effect change. Replacing one person with another largely maintains the status quo if it is done without changing the person's tasks, the technologies used in performing these tasks, or the structure in which the person is inserted. Even if the new person is better qualified, there will be little opportunity to benefit from these new competences except by adjusting tasks, technologies, or authority structures. Similarly, upgrading one information system to another generates little change if the upgrade is not accompanied by changes in tasks, people, or structure. Even if the new system has superior functionality, the organization will benefit little unless the added functionality is utilized to restructure tasks, rebalance people's workload, or revise the command structure.

If an information system is to effect nontrivial change, its implementation team must embrace all four components in Figure 2.1. Hence, organizational implementation is a sociotechnical process. While technical development produces the new technological system, it is for organizational implementation to integrate it in the organization. This integration involves that you configure the system for the organization and configure the organization for the system. As an example of the duration of this process, Pries-Heje and Dittrich (2009) describe how the implementation of an enterprise resource planning (ERP) system lasted 1.5–2 years from when the organization started configuring the ERP system, through user training, to shakedown. Before this process, the organization had spent a year selecting their ERP system. After it, they spent another year on a follow-up project to address more than 500 issues reported during shakedown. It was only after the follow-up project that the organization firmly entered benefits capture.

2.2   EPISODIC VS. CONTINUOUS CHANGE

Pries-Heje and Dittrich's (2009) description of the ERP project reflects an episodic perception of change. Admittedly, the episode is year-long but it is perceived as contained within a temporally bounded project. This perception is typical of the system view on organizational implementation. In contrast, the practice view is rooted in a perception of change as continuous. The difference between episodic and continuous change is analyzed by Weick and Quinn (1999). Table 2.1 provides a summary. It has profound consequences for organizational implementation whether change is perceived as episodic or continuous.

Table 2.1: Episodic and continuous change

	Episodic Change	Continuous Change
Definition	Change is infrequent, discontinuous, and intentional	Change is constant, evolving, and incremental
Perspective	Macro, "an outsider's perspective"	Micro, "an insider's perspective"
Duration	Temporally bounded, "a project"	Open-ended, "a program"
Intervention steps	1. Unfreeze, 2. Change, 3. Refreeze	1. Freeze, 2. Rebalance, 3. Unfreeze
Change agent	Prime mover who effects change	Sense maker who redirects change

Organizational change is often perceived as the three-step process of unfreezing, changing, and refreezing (Weick and Quinn, 1999). That is, organizations are basically stable; they are in a state of equilibrium punctuated by *episodic change*. Without intentional interventions, the equilibrium will keep the organization in a stable state, in which its operations proceed in an unchanging and time-honored manner. The first step in the change process, unfreezing, serves to suspend the forces that keep the equilibrium in place. This preparatory step is necessary to overcome inertia and make change possible. Change, the second step of the process, modifies how work is done by installing new structures and processes. Lastly, refreezing integrates the new way of working in the staff members' understanding of their work. This third step embeds the change in the organization by readjusting the forces that define the state of equilibrium. When this has been achieved, control can be relinquished back to the equilibrium, which will keep the organization in its new stable state. The change episode has come to its end.

From the close-up perspective of someone inside an organization, it tends to be an oversimplification to perceive change as distinct episodes on a background of stability. Rather, the members of an organization experience a process of *continuous change*. While each adaptation and adjustment is small, their frequency makes them capable of gradually changing structures and processes. The adaptations and adjustments do not, however, follow a preconceived plan. As a result, the ensuing change is emergent in the sense that new ways of working come into existence without explicit a priori intentions (Orlikowski, 1996). The absence of preconceived intentions may lead to changes that, in retrospect, are undesirable and call for interventions to redirect the process of change.

Such interventions involve the three steps of freezing, rebalancing, and unfreezing (Weick and Quinn, 1999). First, freezing is necessary to reveal patterns in what is happening. It serves to make room for reflection and intentionality by, temporarily, stepping back from the unceasing adaptations and adjustments. Second, rebalancing is about reinterpreting the patterns in what is happening to remove blockages and reframe selected issues as opportunities. The rebalancing is not taking over from the adaptations and adjustments but reshaping the conditions within which they will unfold henceforth. Third, unfreezing after rebalancing consists of resuming improvisation and continuous change. If the rebalancing has been successful, the adaptations and adjustments will now unfold in ways that are more mindful of the goals promoted by the intervention.

The change agent in episodic and continuous change is a prime mover and a sense maker, respectively. A prime mover is forward-looking and creates change. A sense maker redirects change by retrospectively revealing patterns in what is happening. In addition, the prime mover can be called in to effect change and leave the organization again when the change episode has been completed. That is, the prime mover can, but need not, be an external consultant who is hired for the duration of the change project. In contrast, continuous change implies a need for the sense maker to be present in the organization on a day-to-day basis to be able to react to change as it emerges. That is, the sense maker will typically have a permanent position in the organization, but it need not be a position in change management. The role of sense maker is often informally assumed, rather than formally assigned.

2.3   SINGLE-LOOP VS. DOUBLE-LOOP LEARNING

While the distinction between episodic and continuous change is about the temporality of change, the distinction between single-loop and double-loop learning is about the depth of change. Argyris and Schön (1978) contend that when something goes wrong, the initial reaction of many people is to look for another way to achieve the thwarted goal. That is, they change their approach but do not question the desirability of the goal. This is single-loop learning. It is about how to attain an existing goal while keeping performance within the range specified by existing norms. The search for a solution is restricted to an analysis of how the goal can be attained with different means; see Figure 2.2.

In contrast, double-loop learning returns to the assumptions that gave rise to the goal and asks why it is deemed desirable. By questioning the goal, double-loop learning opens up for a wider range of responses to the current situation. Rather than finding alternative means of attaining the thwarted goal, it may be possible to reformulate the goal. Goal reformulation involves taking a fresh look at deeply seated assumptions, such as norms and values. This is not easy, but may lead to radically new ideas. The attraction of double-loop learning is twofold. First, it provides a possible way out of situations that are unsolvable with single-loop learning. Second, it can lead to grander solutions.

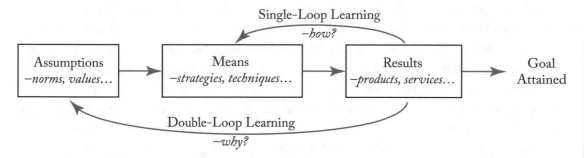

Figure 2.2: Single-loop and double-loop learning, based on Argyris and Schön (1978).

To make informed decisions in dynamic contexts, organizations need a capacity for double-loop learning (Argyris and Schön, 1978). Otherwise, they will be insufficiently agile in their response to changing circumstances and opportunities. However, most people appear mainly to employ single-loop learning. They do not intentionally avoid double-loop learning but behave in ways that make it practically impossible. Argyris and Schön (1978) argue that most people behave defensively when they experience difficulty. Defensive behavior is especially likely among people who mostly succeed—and have a reputation of succeeding—because they have never learned how to learn from failure. Learning from failure is central to double-loop learning, which involves failing to attain the current goal as well as failing to set a goal that could be attained. The defensive behavior that locks people in single-loop learning can be characterized as follows (Argyris and Schön, 1978):

- *Remain in unilateral control*: This involves persuading others about the goals you deem desirable. Thereby, learning is sealed. It remains closed to redefinition by others. The alternative is that people try to develop with others a mutual definition of purposes.

- *Maximize winning and minimize losing:* This involves feeling that once you have decided on your goals, changing them would be admitting defeat. In this way, single-loop learning is the only road to success and double-loop learning is a sign of weakness.

- *Suppress negative feelings:* This involves experiencing negative feelings as an indication of incompetence and, therefore, seeking to avoid situations in which you or others express negative feelings. As a result, ideas are not tested publicly, but merely privately.

- *Be rational:* This involves that interactions should proceed as objective discussions, irrespective of the feelings that may underlie them. Actions should be evaluated by whether they attain defined goals. However, this leads to low freedom of choice, low commitment, and low risk taking.

The purpose of the defensive behavior is to avoid feeling embarrassed, incompetent, and vulnerable. It generates organizations in which people avoid seriously testing the premises, inferences, and conclusions that shape their actions. To encourage double-loop learning, organizations must become more dialogical. That is, they must embrace uncertainty, emphasize mutual influence, exercise open communication, and engage in testing their assumptions in group settings.

Defensive behavior complicates the organizational implementation of information systems because the structural changes necessary for benefits capture involve interrogating norms and other assumptions (Section 2.1). In a retrospective analysis of their approach to integrated organization and technology development, Rohde and Wulf (2018, p. 294) conclude that "many organizations tend to opt for small, easily controllable changes that have no fundamental impact on organizational structure, strategy, or culture." These organizations settle for small benefits to avoid uncertainty, discontinuity, and double-loop learning. Implementation teams often find themselves struggling with the tension between single-loop learning, which is safe but constrained, and double-loop learning, which is uncertain but powerful.

2.4   BUREAUCRATIC VS. ORGANIC ORGANIZATIONS

Information systems are implemented in all forms of organizations. An influential distinction is between bureaucratic and organic organizations (Mintzberg, 1980). This distinction operates at the level of their structural form. In contrast, the distinction between single-loop and double-loop learning operates at the level of the people who work in the organization. Bureaucratic organizations rely on standardization for coordination. They may standardize skills (e.g., hospitals, which hire people with formalized educational backgrounds), work processes (e.g., mass production firms, which formalize processes to create repeated routines), or outputs (e.g., divisionalized firms, which impose performance standards on their divisions). Organic organizations, by contrast, achieve coordination through direct supervision (e.g., entrepreneurial firms, in which the chief executive oversees everyone else) or mutual adjustment (e.g., consulting firms, which fuse experts from different specialties into self-governing project teams).

Bureaucratic and organic organizations differ in their readiness for change. *Bureaucratic organizations* tend to be large. Standardization enables them to be large and efficient at the same time. To get to this point, they have invested much time and effort in fine-tuning, and they continuously attend to whether standards are met. These organizations are tailored for effective and efficient performance under stable conditions; they react slowly to changing circumstances. Implementing a new information system in a bureaucratic organization can be a long and formal process that involves modifying interrelated, time-honored standards. The primary focus in this process will likely be on planned change, while emergent change is considered secondary or seen as a threat to standard compliance.

Organic organizations favor flexibility over continuity. They seek to be effective by investing continual effort in matching their environment rather than in standardizing their internal structures. That is, they are geared toward dynamic environments. To remain flexible, they are typically smaller than bureaucratic organizations. In organic organizations, emergent change is embraced. As a result, organizational implementation is less heavy in up-front planning and more about responding quickly and relevantly to changes and opportunities when they occur. This difference in focus involves shifting resources from preparations and shakedown toward implementation activities during continued use. For this to be practically possible, the technology must be extensively configurable and not require extensive training. Such technologies have been labeled lightweight (Bygstad, 2017).

CHAPTER 3

Technology Adoption: Boosters and Barriers

While the previous chapter elaborated the rationale for organizations to implement information systems, this chapter explores the reasons for success, trouble, and failure in organizational implementation. These reasons are many and interdependent. They include reasons about the technology as such, but they are mostly about the fit between the system and organization. Different groups of people in the organization will perceive this fit differently. They may, for example, assign primacy to different aspects of the organizational change pursued with the implementation and, as a result, disagree about whether the change is desirable. Such disagreements can lead some groups to embrace the system, others to adopt it hesitantly, and still others to work around it.

This chapter starts by distinguishing between adoption at the management level and user level (Section 3.1). The management-level decision to adopt a system leads to the formation of an implementation team, which organizes the user-level adoption. At both levels, adoption is a sociotechnical process influenced by facts as well as feelings. Navigating this process requires appreciation of the factors that boost adoption and the barriers that thwart it. The boosters of adoption concern all four components of organizational change, that is, people, technology, tasks, and structure (Section 3.2). The barriers to adoption include lack of urgency, going solid, change fatigue, and counterimplementation (Section 3.3).

3.1 ADOPTION AT THE MANAGEMENT AND USER LEVELS

The adoption of technology by organizations is a two-stage process that consists of primary adoption at the managerial level followed by secondary adoption at the staff level (Gallivan, 2001). Figure 3.1 illustrates the process.

The first stage involves that management experiences a need for organizational change, identifies a technology that promises to facilitate this change, and decides to adopt it. This management adoption process precedes organizational implementation. If the technology is an off-the-shelf product, then the organization can proceed straight to purchase and implementation. If the technology has to be custom made, then its technical development must take place before the organization can proceed to implementation.

The second stage is the actual implementation, which includes the full or partial adoption of the technology by individual users. Management may take three approaches to secondary adoption. They can (1) make it mandatory, (2) recommend and advocate it without mandating it, or (3) leave it a voluntary option. Irrespective of the approach taken, secondary adoption involves that individual users and groups form their own opinions about the technology and their inclination to adopt it. Multiple studies have shown that mandating adoption provides no guarantee that users actually adopt (e.g., Aarts et al., 2004; Bhattacherjee et al., 2018; Granlien and Hertzum, 2012; Yeung et al., 2012).

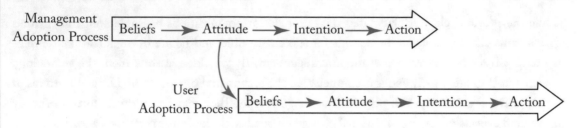

Figure 3.1: The two-stage process of technology adoption in organizations.

The non-adoption of mandated systems brings out a crucial feature of the two-stage adoption process: The beliefs and attitudes that drive intention and action at the two levels may differ to the point of resulting in contradictory actions (Bhattacherjee et al., 2018). Management has an organization-level perspective and will be driven by beliefs about whether the system will benefit the organization as a whole. However, there may be user groups that do not benefit. Frequently, the adoption of a new system entails that some users are tasked with additional work to enter or process information, while other users reap the benefits that accrue from this additional work (Grudin, 1994). The users who benefit will often be in managerial positions; their perception of the system will mainly be shaped by its benefits. In contrast, those who are tasked with additional work, or fear being made redundant, will perceive the system as a burden and may oppose its implementation.

The uneven distribution of work and benefits means that the implementation team needs to put care and effort into its communication about the new system. In particular, you should not assume that primary adoption is a sufficient precondition for secondary adoption to ensue. Management commitment to the new system is one of the most important things to communicate (Petter et al., 2013; Sabherwal et al., 2006; Shao et al., 2016). Unless management puts its weight behind the system, the implementation team will lack the mandate and power necessary to overcome barriers and drive the process forward. In large organizations, the adoption process may involve intermediate stages in between primary and secondary adoption, thereby resulting in interrelated adoption processes at, for example, management, division, workgroup, and user levels (Gallivan, 2001). Such intermediate stages create further possibilities for cross-stage contradictions and increase the risk of ambiguous communication.

At the user level, adoption is governed by the organizational implementation process and proceeds through preparations, initial use, and continued use. At least, that is the managerial intention. In practice, adoption tends to deviate from a smooth progression through preparations, initial use, and continued use. For example, Fichman and Kemerer (1999) argue that adoption is often delayed, shallow, or scattered, thereby resulting in gaps between planned and actual adoption. Even when adoption is mandated, the actual result is more often partial than full adoption (Jeyaraj and Sabherwal, 2008). The partiality may occur early as well as late in the process and it can even amount to non-use; see Figure 3.2. The different kinds of partiality and non-use occur for different reasons and, therefore, point to different risks in the implementation process (Soliman and Rinta-Kahila, 2020). You need different countermeasures in working to avoid these risks:

- *Refusal* happens before use on the basis of expectations about what using the new system will be like. An important means in working to avoid refusal is expectation management.

- *Rejection* happens shortly after go-live on the basis of initial experiences with the new system. Important means in avoiding rejection are user training and a well-managed shakedown phase.

- *Discontinuance* happens after a period of continued use and suggests that changes in tasks or structures have rendered the system out of date. To avoid premature discontinuance, the organization must maintain the system through a permanent readiness to assess and act on revision requests.

- *Partial adoption and use* resemble rejection and discontinuance, but at a smaller scale. It is merely parts of the system and associated procedures that are rejected or discontinued, not the entire system. While the means of avoiding partial adoption and use are similar to those of avoiding rejection and discontinuance, the smaller scale makes partiality more likely to go unnoticed.

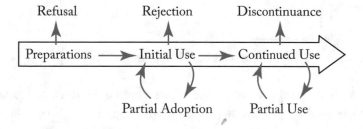

Figure 3.2: User-level technology adoption.

While management has an interest in complete and continued adoption, users have an—equally valid—interest in avoiding the use of a system they deem inconvenient, disruptive, or even harmful. Carnevale (2003) contends that because organizational change is fundamentally about altering the dynamics of social systems, "it is inevitable and natural that conflict is constantly in play when individuals, groups, and the organization try to come to terms with change." The implementation team is pivotal to the successful handling of these conflicts and tensions.

3.2   BOOSTERS OF ADOPTION

Numerous studies have searched for the factors that boost adoption and, thereby, facilitate successful implementation. An influential framework in these studies is the technology acceptance model (Davis et al., 1989; Venkatesh and Davis, 2000; Venkatesh et al., 2003). It aims to explain whether an individual person will adopt an information system. In its original formulation, the technology acceptance model posited that individual adoption is determined by perceived usefulness and perceived ease of use (Davis et al., 1989). That is, adoption is essentially a cost/benefit assessment in which the person considers whether the benefits of adopting the system (its perceived usefulness) outweigh the costs associated with using it (its perceived ease of use). According to the model, the person's perceptions of usefulness and ease of use determine the person's attitude toward using the system, which in turn determines whether the person forms an intention to use the system and actually starts using it; see Figure 3.3. Studies find that the effect of perceived usefulness on intention is stronger and more long-lasting than that of perceived ease of use (King and He, 2006; Venkatesh and Davis, 2000).

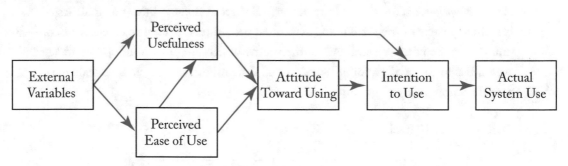

Figure 3.3: The technology acceptance model, based on Davis et al. (1989).

Perceived usefulness and perceived ease of use are beliefs. Thus, technology acceptance is determined by the individual person's beliefs about the system, not by the system as such. The beliefs are shaped by external variables, but different people may form different beliefs about the introduction of the same system in the same organization. The technology acceptance model asserts that the only way to boost the adoption of a system is by improving people's beliefs about its cost-effectiveness. Any external variable influences adoption only indirectly by influencing perceived usefulness or perceived ease of use. The model also asserts that perceived ease of use influences perceived usefulness. That is, an easier-to-use system is perceived as more useful—it has a better cost/benefit ratio.

Later revisions of the technology acceptance model have extended it in various ways. Three of these revisions appear particularly important because they have modified the fundamental features of the original model. First, its individual perspective has been softened by the introduction of *social influence* as a factor with a direct effect on intention to use. Social influence is about whether a person perceives that important others believe that the person should adopt the system (Venkatesh et al., 2003). Such beliefs are for example conveyed in organizational norms. The effect of social influence on intention to use is stronger when use is mandatory (Venkatesh et al., 2003) and may disappear altogether when use is voluntary (Venkatesh and Davis, 2000).

Second, the utilitarian perspective of the original model has been supplemented with an acknowledgment of the influence of *perceived enjoyment* on system adoption. Perceived enjoyment is about whether a person likes to use a system in its own right, apart from any performance consequences associated with its use (Davis et al., 1992). Fun, joy, pleasure, and the like are important to organizational life; work is not just about performance. Hornbæk and Hertzum (2017) find that the effect of perceived enjoyment on the intention to use a system is about as large as the effects of perceived usefulness and perceived ease of use.

Third, the organizational support for the system has become explicitly represented in the model, thereby changing its otherwise context-independent appearance. Organizational support, also referred to as *facilitating conditions*, concerns whether a person believes that an organizational and technical infrastructure exists to support the use of the system. When people believe so, they are more likely to adopt the system; this effect appears to be particularly strong for older staff (Venkatesh et al., 2003).

A consistent finding across the studies of organizational implementation is that no one single factor is sufficient to ensure success (Petter et al., 2013). This finding complicates implementation efforts because it means that you need to maintain a diversified focus on multiple, nontrivial, and interdependent factors. That said, a limited number of factors have consistently been found to boost adoption; see Table 3.1. These factors, reviewed by Petter et al. (2013), incorporate those of the technology acceptance model and concern all four components in Figure 2.1: people, technology, tasks, and structure.

Several of the *people* factors are about personal traits and previous experiences. These factors include attitude toward technology, technology experience, and self-efficacy. It is largely impossible for the implementation team to effect change in these factors, but communication and user training are important in dealing with them. In addition, they emphasize the importance of selecting the right people for participation in implementation activities. Rasmussen et al. (2011) find that the users selected for participation in IT projects are more often selected for their ability to champion the organizational implementation than for being representative of their user colleagues. Such champions have a positive attitude toward technology and a catching belief that they can master it. The implementation team can mostly influence two of the people factors: trust and expectations. Aligning expectations with the actual costs and benefits of adopting the system makes for a much smoother process. The importance of enjoyment reiterates that it would be misconstrued to focus exclusively on cost-effectiveness (Gerow et al., 2013). It would also be misconstrued to perceive enjoyment merely as a task-unrelated extra; people enjoy being creative, feeling empowered, and various other task-related experiences (Amabile et al., 2005; Fisher, 2010). Finally, organizational role is important to adoption. This factor shows that many systems distribute work and benefits unevenly across staff groups and that this uneven distribution influences some groups' inclination to adopt (Grudin, 1994).

Table 3.1: Factors that have consistently been found to influence whether the organizational decision to implement an information system is followed by adoption at the user level, based on Petter et al. (2013)

Factor	Description
People	
Attitudes toward technology	Degree to which people have a favorable view about technology
Technology experience	Amount of past experience a person has had with technology, even if it is a different type of technology than the system considered for adoption
Self-efficacy	People's self-confidence about their ability to master technology
Trust	Degree to which people have a positive view about the system in terms of it being used in their best interest
User expectations	Degree to which people's early perceptions about the system are consistent with the ways in which it changes their work when put into operation
Enjoyment	Level of pleasure or joy that people derive from using the system
Organizational role	Person's position within the organization, such as manager, secretary, etc.
Technology	
System quality	Quality of the system, such as its ease of use, flexibility, reliability, and response time
Information quality	Quality of the system outputs, such as their accuracy, completeness, relevance, and understandability

Tasks	
Task compatibility	Fit or consistency between the task and the system
Task difficulty	Degree to which the task supported by the system is challenging for the user
Structure	
Management commitment	Degree to which management puts it weight behind the system as its champion, sponsor, or promoter
Management processes	Policies and procedures used by management to achieve IT alignment and to oversee the implementation and use of the system
Organizational competence	Knowledge possessed by the organization about the implementation and use of IT
Domain expert knowledge	Knowledge level of those who provide the expertise regarding the requirements for the system
Extrinsic motivation	Incentives and rewards (financial, recognition, or reputation) offered by management to encourage staff to use the system
User participation	Degree to which users are involved in the decisions and processes about configuring and implementing the system
Relationship with developers	Nature of the interaction, or closeness, between the developers/configurators and the users of the system
Support quality	Quality of the service that users receive from the IT support staff
IT infrastructure	Suitability and sophistication of the IT infrastructure within the organization

The *technology* factors that boost adoption are about the system and about the outputs from the system. A system is more likely to be adopted if it is easy to use, flexible, reliable, fast, and generates outputs that are accurate, complete, relevant, and understandable (DeLone and McLean, 2003; Petter et al., 2013). System flexibility plays a special role. Without flexibility, you cannot adapt the system to the organization. All adaptations must instead be in the form of the organization adapting to the system—by either complying with the system or working around it. The importance of flexibility increases with the scope of the system and the duration for which it is in operational use:

- For systems with a wide scope, flexibility helps avoid refusal and rejection by allowing you to configure the systems for organization-specific workflows, department-specific priorities, and other local circumstances. Without these possibilities for up-front configuration, the wide scope of the systems would cause an excessive number of misfits between the system and the local practices (Haines, 2009).

- For systems with a long operational life, flexibility helps avoid premature discontinuance by giving you the possibility to reconfigure the systems over time to fit new circumstances that could not be anticipated at go-live. Many systems are in operational use for years or even decades. These systems either evolve considerably over time through reconfiguration or they increasingly restrict the possibilities for organizations to evolve (Hertzum et al., 1993).

The *task* factors that boost adoption are compatibility and difficulty. Higher compatibility and lower difficulty increase the likelihood of adoption. A widespread distinction in understanding task difficulty is between uncertain and equivocal tasks (Daft and Lengel, 1986). Uncertain tasks are characterized by a lack of information (the question is known but the answer is not). Equivocal tasks are characterized by a lack of understanding (the question and answer are both unknown). While uncertain tasks represent situations in which single-loop learning is sufficient, equivocal tasks may require double-loop learning, extensive consultation with more experienced colleagues, or both. Uncertain tasks are simpler than equivocal tasks. They are simpler to perform and it is also simpler to specify what a system should look like to fit an uncertain task than an equivocal task. That is, lower task difficulty makes it easier to achieve high task compatibility. Conversely, high task difficulty is often accompanied by systems with poor task compatibility for at least some aspects of the tasks.

The *structure* factors that boost adoption range from management commitment to IT infrastructure (Table 3.1). Management plays a key role in organizational implementation by putting its weight behind the system, putting processes in place for its implementation, building organizational competence in IT implementation, and incentivizing system use. While incentives such as financial rewards and organizational recognition foster extrinsic motivation (Ryan and Deci, 2000), user participation in the implementation activities foster buy-in and intrinsic motivation (Markus and Mao, 2004). Another outcome of user participation is more and closer interactions between the users and the implementation team. Such interactions further increase the likelihood of adoption. Finally, adoption is facilitated by a technical IT infrastructure that integrates well with the new information system.

3.3   BARRIERS TO ADOPTION

To some extent, barriers to adoption are the flip side of the boosters of adoption. The absence of management commitment and the absence of task compatibility are examples of barriers to adoption, whereas their presence boosts adoption. Thus, Table 3.1 can also be read as a list of major barriers to adoption. It is, however, not all factors that are barriers when absent and boosters when present. For example, the IT infrastructure constitutes a barrier when it is inadequate, but an adequate IT infrastructure is mainly the absence of this barrier, not a factor that actively boosts adoption. In contrast, influence on the new system through participation in the implementation process boosts adoption, but the absence of participation is mainly the absence of this boost, not the presence of an active barrier to adoption. In their seminal study of people's motivation to work, Herzberg et al. (1959) argue that most factors are either barriers or boosters (hygienes or motivators, respectively, in their terminology).

Four distinct barriers to adoption are lack of urgency, going solid, change fatigue, and counterimplementation. Many troubled and failed organizational implementations have struggled with these four barriers (e.g., Arvidsson et al., 2014; Fitzgerald et al., 2014; Garside, 2004; Hertzum and Simonsen, 2020; Keen, 1981; Müller et al., 2017). They capture conditions that are sufficiently common to warrant close attention and sufficiently unyielding to be potential showstoppers.

Lack of urgency is the sense that there is no need for change. It arises out of contentment with the status quo and fosters preservation of the status quo. When people are basically content with the current state of affairs, they tend to see change as effortful and risky rather than engaging and rewarding. Any change involves effort and risk. For example, the resources devoted to achieving change are taken away from other activities, which may suffer. Thus, many arguments for being cautious are perfectly valid. It makes good sense to analyze the risks carefully, substantiate opportunities with data, not act on whims, and so forth. In short, arguments for being cautious can be forcefully made. If they are made in a climate characterized by lack of urgency, then most change initiatives suffocate (Fitzgerald et al., 2014; Hertzum and Simonsen, 2020).

Kotter (2008) argues that lack of urgency can take two forms: complacency and anxiety. Complacency means that you see no real problem in the current state of affairs or that you see problems but do not feel that they call for changes on your part. There may be a need for change but it involves other people in the organization, not you. When the need is deflected in this way, change does not happen because there is no agent to drive it. Anxiety produces the same result but in a very different way. Anxiety ensues when you are insecure about the current state of affairs. In contrast to complacency, anxiety often leads to frenetic activity but these activities are defensive in that they aim at preserving the current state of affairs to avoid losses. The high level of activity can be mistaken for an expression that change is urgently needed. It is rather an expression that change is unwelcome.

Large change initiatives such as the implementation of information systems are typically motivated by a business case, which provides facts and figures to demonstrate that the benefits of the system outweigh the costs and risks. Through analysis and logic, business cases talk to people's intellect. Thereby, they largely fail to address complacency and anxiety, which are first and foremost feelings. Even if the analysis and logic are sound, they are dull instruments for reducing complacency and anxiety. To be effective, you must combine the analysis and logic with means that help people experience the new system as exciting and meaningful. By doing so, you create a determination to make the change happen—a sense of urgency (Kotter, 2008). Once people have enthusiastically embraced a goal beyond the status quo, they work hard to overcome the obstacles involved in achieving it. Without the sense of urgency, the obstacles multiply and the goal does not seem worth the hassle.

Going solid is the state in which an organization operates at such high efficiency that all staff resources are committed to tasks that are necessary for the organization to function at its current level of production (Cook and Rasmussen, 2005). This state is the result of tight budgets combined with modern management techniques that have allowed organizations to reduce operational inefficiencies. However, it is also a substantial barrier to systems adoption. Going solid is a barrier to adoption because it has the unfortunate side effect that there are no resources for the extra work involved in adopting a new system and integrating it into work practices. Without such resource buffers, the organization is locked in its current way of operating; it has become largely incapable of change.

All organizations experience instances during which they temporarily go solid. The last few weeks before a major deadline is a common example. Go-live dates for new information systems should be scheduled to avoid such periods. However, some organizations have gone solid in a more chronic way. In fiercely competitive markets with small profit margins, organizations may not be able to afford resource buffers. The staff will be acutely aware of this condition, often through the presence of demanding work-output targets. Under such conditions, there are neither resources nor incentives for the staff to engage in discussions about how a new information system may enable them to do their work differently or better (Arvidsson et al., 2014; Orlikowski, 2000). On the contrary, any disturbance caused by a new system and any requirement for changing time-honored procedures is primarily experienced as a threat to upholding performance levels.

If an organization goes solid, then risk aversion ensues. You tend to be risk averse when you perceive that running the risk will have a low probability of paying off (Holt and Laury, 2002). When all available resources are needed to meet performance targets, then staff will experience change as a daunting challenge. Because change is deemed nearly unachievable, it becomes something to avoid (Arvidsson et al., 2014): The probability of success is seen as too low to justify the effort of trying. Refusal and rejection may be avoided, but organizational implementation under these conditions is likely to result in partial adoption and partial use. Specifically, the patterns of use will tend to congeal before the full potential of the system has been realized because staff is eager to return to the directly productive activities and, thus, disinclined to engage in design-in-use activities (Tyre and Orlikowski, 1994).

Change fatigue is a reaction to overly frequent change. The dynamic circumstances that foster change fatigue are the near opposite of those in which organizations go solid. While going solid is a barrier to adoption in fairly stable environments, change fatigue is a barrier to adoption in dynamic environments where constant organization-external changes necessitate frequent organization-internal adaptations. If all the internal changes were clearly linked to the external events that caused them, then the changes would have purpose and logic. But with the large number of changes, the links are blurred and the purpose and logic of the changes become unclear to those who should adopt them. The resulting attitude is not unwillingness to change, but a sense of randomness and fatigue (McMillan and Perron, 2013). Reporting about change fatigue among healthcare clinicians, Garside (2004, p. 90) captures it eloquently:

> Clinicians want to change things for the better for their patients and for working practices. They perceive an endless stream of initiatives, see many of them "fail" and reappear with a new name, see conflicting directions of change, and a plethora of initiatives so great that they fail to see the final purpose or connecting logic. They believe that "managerialism" has eroded their autonomy. What is probably more important is that they do not have the space or the time in which to pursue these programs.

Change fatigue is fueled by the experience that many change initiatives are ineffective. However, demanding a higher success rate is not a realistic cure. Succeeding in dynamic environments is much more about learning from failure than avoiding it (Scott and Vessey, 2000). The best cure against change fatigue is, probably, to reduce the number of change initiatives and clarify their purpose and logic. The former is a top-management decision outside the purview of any single implementation process, the latter is within the control of the individual implementation team and should be at the core of its communication efforts. With fewer, better-motivated change initiatives competing for the staff's attention, each initiative becomes more convincing and digestible. In addition, you should plan each initiative with an eye to obtaining early benefits, which help create and maintain momentum.

Counterimplementation is a deliberate attempt to thwart the implementation of a new system (Keen, 1981). That is, counterimplementation has active opposition as its core element. This element sets counterimplementation apart from lack of urgency (at least in its complacency form), going solid, and change fatigue. There can be many valid reasons for opposing a new system, including that "many innovations are dumb ideas" (Keen, 1981, p. 27). The system view (Figure 1.2) is driven by the conviction that implementing the system will be beneficial for the organization. The large number of organizational implementations that fail to produce benefits shows that this conviction is often questionable or plain wrong. In these cases, it is in the best interest of the organization to heed the opposition raised against the system. However, opposition is often perceived as a barrier for proceeding with the planned change rather than as an opportunity for learning.

Another reason for counterimplementation is that the system threatens the interests of individuals or groups within the organization by limiting their autonomy, reducing their influence, eroding their position, or adding to their workload. These individuals and groups may all try to act in the interest of the organization, but they often have disparate definitions of exactly what that is. Obviously, the line between opposing a dumb idea and acting in self-interest is open to discussion and disagreement. Because counterimplementation tends to be unwelcome, it can be risky to engage in overt opposition. Therefore, counterimplementation is frequently exercised by indirect means, such as by diverting resources, deflecting goals, and dissipating energies (Bardach, 1977). Examples of these strategies include the following (Keen, 1981).

- *"Make sure we're in charge and don't let outsiders cause trouble; take it slowly."* This strategy consists of taking charge of the implementation activities—apparently a supportive move—and then letting them drag out. It diverts resources by reducing the intensity of the implementation activities. Without a person in charge who drives the process forward, it likely grinds to a halt.

- *"Let's do it right!"* This strategy deflects the goal of the implementation activities by piling on additional activities to ensure that everything is done right—apparently a supportive intention. This way, the implementation activities swell up and become too diffuse and extensive to see through to completion.

- *"We're certainly interested and we'll be happy to provide some inputs, but…"* This strategy emphasizes that while the new system is in principle a good idea, the local circumstances in the organization make the system unfit for this particular situation. It dissipates energies by distancing the actor from the system and creating an option to withdraw if the system gets into trouble (*"I told you so"*).

The counterimplementation strategies rely on expressing token support as a pretext for introducing complications and delays. They exploit ambiguity about what the new system should help achieve and how it should be implemented. If you reduce such ambiguity, you also reduce the possibilities for individuals and groups to apply the counterimplementation strategies. In addition, the strategies are particularly effective when applied by people in powerful positions (Müller et al., 2017; Nilsen et al., 2019). If these people can be brought on board by means of incentives or other boosters, then the implementation team has removed a large barrier to adoption.

CHAPTER 4

Implementing Information Systems: Three Phases

Information systems do not change organizations in ways that are predetermined by the technology. If they did, their organizational implementation would have a fixed outcome once the managerial adoption process (Figure 3.1) had resulted in a decision to adopt. Rather, the organization that implements a new system adapts it to the organization as well as adapts the organization to it. This mutual adaptation makes organizational implementation a design process. Simon (1996, p. 111) says that "everyone designs who devises courses of action aimed at changing existing situations into preferred ones." What is devised through organizational implementation are new, IT-enabled ways of working—that is, organizational change.

Design is neither restricted to technical development, nor does it end at go-live. It continues throughout technical development and organizational implementation. What changes at go-live is the relation between design and use (Bjögvinsson et al., 2012; Germonprez et al., 2011). Before go-live, use is an imagined future—captured in visions and modeled in descriptions. Design is directed at this imagined future, which has not yet been experienced and therefore remains somewhat fluid and abstract. While it is yet unknown what use will really be like, it is increasingly manifest what the system will be like. The technical developers are completing more and more of the system functionality. Or the functionality has been determined by the decision about which off-the-shelf system to purchase. After go-live, use is experienced and, thus, becomes salient and concrete. When use becomes salient and concrete, it overrides the models and descriptions of use. Design choices and system functionality can no longer simply be justified by references to the models and descriptions. Instead, design must contend with actual use.

Organizational implementation is prepared before go-live but acted out after go-live (Shaul and Tauber, 2013). It is a design-in-use process in the double sense that it takes place in the context of use and is informed by actual use. As a design-in-use process, organizational implementation continues design during shakedown immediately after go-live and during the long, subsequent process of benefits capture. That is, the work of the implementation team proceeds in three phases.

- *Preparations*, which consist of planning the activities initiated by the decision to adopt the system. Temporally, the preparations overlap with the technical finalization of the system. This overlap creates possibilities for influencing system finalization. However, it also creates challenges because there may not be a stable basis for revising work procedures and conducting user training.

- *Going live*, which is the initial, planned change. This phase starts when the users begin to use the system for performing their tasks. It is at this point that the system and its consequences become salient to the organization. In spite of the preparations, go-live is a hectic phase, which many users experience as uncertain or frustrating. It should preferably be brief.

- *Continuing design during use*, which is a long, improvisational process. By using the system, new opportunities emerge. Some users will seize these opportunities by customizing the system, changing their ways of working, and showing their colleagues the results. Other opportunities will be triggered by external events or require organizational support for their realization.

Collectively, the three phases blend planned change with improvisational change, but any single organizational implementation may emphasize one or the other. Kræmmergaard and Rose (2002) describe the implementation of an off-the-shelf system following a process that emphasized planned change. Change was issued top-down and the intention was to implement the entire change all at once. The implementation team had a representative from each department and a strong mandate from the steering committee. In spite of about a year of preparations, go-live resulted in three months of hectic activity during which the communication between the implementation team and steering committee became tense. Furthermore, the collaboration with the super users was challenged by the large number of implementation issues that were brought to the super users' attention by frustrated users. In the continued process, the head of the implementation team was changed from a technical manager to a business manager to reflect the changing focus of the implementation activities. When the organization started to benefit from the system, the members and collaborators of the implementation team were gradually relocated back to their departments.

Rasmussen et al. (2010) describe a contrasting case, which emphasized improvisational change. This case followed an agile process. As a result, technical development and organizational implementation were tightly coupled and most of the activity happened after go-live. The implementation team was headed by a manager from business development and had representatives from department management, users, and the vendor. During the preparations, the implementation team trained the super users in configuring the system and the users in using its base functionality. At go-live, the system with base functionality was released and the implementation team and super users started promoting its possibilities for growing in accordance with local needs. The continued process lasted a couple of years and consisted of (1) collecting input for new modules to be iteratively added to the system, (2) designing, developing, and releasing new system modules, and (3) adapting procedures to the evolving system. In this process, the implementation team collaborated extensively with the vendor and super users.

The implementation process described by Rasmussen et al. (2010) was incremental. Each new module constituted an increment that extended the system and had its own go-live date. This way, the continued process after the base system went live effectively contained additional iterations of the three implementation phases. By iterating the phases for each new module, the implementation was broken into smaller steps that were tailored to the evolving use of the system. With smaller steps, each iteration required fewer preparations, go-live was less hectic, and so forth. However, the issues covered by each phase remained the same from one iteration to the next.

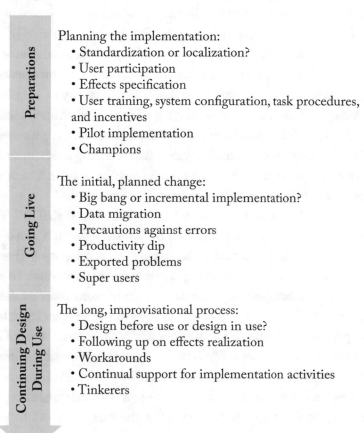

Figure 4.1: The three phases of organizational implementation. Chapters 5–7 elaborate the issues listed for each phase.

Figure 4.1 provides an overview of the issues central to each phase. These issues will be elaborated in Chapters 5–7. An overarching theme in these issues is that the implementation team has a different key collaborator in each phase. The different key collaborators illustrate the focus of each phase. During preparations, champions serve a key role by putting their weight behind the system to raise expectations, build momentum, and create buy-in. During go-live, the super users provide essential support and act as safeguards against errors. During continued use, the tinkerers among the users explore ways of improving organizational outputs and processes by seizing the possibilities afforded by the system.

Often, the people in charge of organizational implementation are different from those in charge of technical development. This separation of responsibilities tends to create an unfortunate gap between technical developers who are not involved in how the system is received by users and organizational implementers who have little influence on the system (Hertzum and Simonsen, 2011; Leonardi, 2009). That is, the gap impoverishes the mutual adaptation of organization and system. To succeed with mutual adaptation, the system must remain adaptable also after it has gone live. This requires that development resources are available to the implementation team. If the system has extensive configuration facilities, these resources can mostly be used for configuring the system. Otherwise, they will be needed for developing additional or revised functionality.

Rohde and Wulf (2018) find that technical-development managers are aware that technology leads to organizational changes, but also that they are often unwilling to acknowledge this explicitly in their plans. These managers perceive organizational change as associated with tensions that will complicate their work. By making their plans exclusively about technical development, they seek to avoid addressing and surfacing these tensions. Relatedly, Markus and Keil (1994) note that technical-development units are usually not held accountable for whether the systems they deliver are adopted by users and lead to the benefits that motivated their development. These studies suggest that many technical developers shy away from organizational implementation. To some extent, their reluctance to engage in organizational implementation mirrors many users' reluctance to engage in organizational implementation—because they do not experience an urgent need, have all their time committed to their primary work, and so forth. For both developers and users, an additional reason for their reluctance may be uncertainty about how to approach organizational implementation.

The three next chapters aim to reduce such uncertainty by explaining the activities involved in organizational implementation. It is the responsibility of the implementation team to organize these activities. By way of summarizing the preceding chapters, Table 4.1 lists questionable assumptions about organizational implementation. Realizing that these assumptions are questionable, often untenable, is the first step in understanding and mastering organizational implementation.

Table 4.1: Questionable assumptions about organizational implementation. In all organizational implementations, some of these assumptions are untenable; in some organizational implementations, all of them are untenable

Questionable Assumptions
• Organizations are prepared to change, including by learning from their failures and by questioning their time-honored ways of doing and thinking
• Once the managerial adoption process has resulted in a decision to adopt, it can be assumed that management is committed to the system and will champion its adoption
• Organizational implementation is about technically installing the system and training the users in operating its user interface; the rest will happen by itself
• Organizational implementation is about replacing one system, or manual procedure, with a new system; the organizational ramifications should be few and small
• For the users, organizational implementation involves starting to work in compliance with new procedures; it is not an engaged process of devising new practices
• At go-live, everybody has bought into the new system and the organizational changes associated with it, even those who do not themselves benefit from the system and changes
• Barriers to adoption are essentially irrational; the organization will benefit from adopting and using the system as is
• Technical development ends at go-live and, for that reason, technical developers need not concern themselves with organizational implementation
• Organizational implementation ends when the system has gone live and the hectic shake-down period immediately after go-live has come to its end

CHAPTER 5

Preparations: Planning the Implementation

Organizational implementation involves changing the work configuration. The new system needs to be configured for the organization; the staff needs new competences to use the system; tasks need to be revised; the revised tasks need to be incorporated in how staff construes and performs their work; organizational structures need to be realigned with the new ways of working; and these changes must be aligned with each other. Accomplishing this coordinated change takes careful preparations. These preparations start when the management adoption process has resulted in a decision to adopt and they last until go-live. Because the preparations precede go-live, they can influence the technical finalization of the system but you also have to contend with the risk of not having the final system ready for activities such as user training.

This chapter starts by juxtaposing two ends that must be reconciled in the preparation phase of organizational implementations: standardization and localization (Section 5.1). The tension between these two ends cannot be removed; it is inherent in discussions and decisions about what the organization wants from its new information system. User participation (Section 5.2) and effects specification (Section 5.3) are important instruments in these discussion and decisions. Once made, the decisions must be implemented. In terms of preparations, this involves user training, system configuration, new procedures, and incentives (Section 5.4). Yet, uncertainty about the decisions and preparations cannot be avoided. To test whether to proceed with go-live, a pilot implementation may be performed (Section 5.5). The chapter closes with a discussion of champions (Section 5.6). They are the key collaborators of the implementation team in the preparation phase.

5.1 STANDARDIZATION OR LOCALIZATION?

Organizational implementation involves adapting the system and organization to each other. However, the balance between system adaptations and organizational adaptations varies widely across organizational implementations. At one end of the spectrum, information systems are used as drivers, or catalysts, of changes that enforce new ways of working. These ways of working may be considered best practice, may be required by law, may be part of obtaining industry certification, or may be introduced to simplify workflows by making them similar across the organization. This approach reflects a strategic focus on standardizing organizational practices. At the other end of the spectrum, information systems are implemented to provide better support for current practices.

These practices may already comply with standards, may be specific to organizational units, may vary from case to case for good situational reasons, or may leave many decisions to the users' professional judgment. This approach reflects a main focus on localization—on adapting the system to the organization.

Decisions about when to standardize and when to localize are crucial to how the organizational implementation changes the organization and is experienced by its staff (Malaurent and Avison, 2016; Rolland and Monteiro, 2002). Standardization can be both overdone and underdone. For example, Janssen et al. (2013) studied the implementation of a new electronic-document standard to harmonize the definitions used in the financial reporting from businesses to the Dutch government. Even though the standard was estimated to save Dutch businesses hundreds of millions of euro each year in reduced administrative work, its adoption remained slow and troubled because the businesses did not buy in to the need for the standard. In contrast, McGinn et al. (2011) report that physicians and healthcare managers often mention a lack of uniform standards—at levels from local, through regional, to national—as a barrier to their adoption of electronic health records.

Localization can also be both overdone and underdone. When overdone, the implementation loses its strategic aim and becomes the replacement of one system with another without accompanying organizational change. Little strategic benefit is realized from such implementations (e.g., Arvidsson et al., 2014). In addition, the cost of making extensive localizations may deplete the implementation budget and leave insufficient resources for adaptations during the phases that follow after the preparation phase (Haines, 2009). When systems are insufficiently localized, they fit the users' tasks and context poorly. For example, systems originally developed for use in one country may need considerable localization before they fit the tasks, legal requirements, and cultural context of organizations in another country (Kwahk and Ahn, 2010).

Management and the system vendor often lean more toward standardization than the users, who lean toward localization. In this way, decisions about when to standardize and localize are intermixed with these stakeholders' other interests. For management, standardization is a means of pursuing strategic goals, emphasizing organization-wide issues, and exercising centralized control at the expense of local discretion. Sustained management involvement is required to realize strategic goals (Arvidsson et al., 2014; Ward and Daniel, 2012). For the vendor, standardization means less work to adapt the system to the client organization and better chances that system functionality can subsequently be reused in bids for other contracts. As a consequence, localizations tend to have a price tag. From the users' point of view, standardization tends to oversimplify work by emphasizing its regularities and to under-recognize the number of exceptions to these regularities (Suchman, 2007). The users' detailed knowledge of their work makes them keenly aware of the rich variety of special cases and local particulars. To be useful, the system must take these cases and particulars into account—it must be localized. Otherwise, the users will experience the system as too rigid and find that standardization erodes their decision-making authority (Maas et al., 2014).

The duration of the preparation phase depends on the number of decisions that have to be made about what and how to standardize or localize. For systems as extensive as ERP systems, the implementation team will have to make thousands of such decisions because it is necessary to analyze processes throughout the organization to establish if they should be standardized, changed in other ways, or remain unchanged (Hertzum and Ellingsen, 2019). As a result, it is not unusual that the preparation phase for an extensive implementation spans a year in large organizations (Santamaría-Sánchez et al., 2010). In small and medium-sized organizations, it is considerably briefer (Adam and O'Doherty, 2004). However, many organizations are not intimately understanding their processes, even after the preparation phase. As a result, they may have to pause their system rollouts during go-live to revisit process issues, decide the extent of system and organizational adaptation, and then resume the go-live phase.

5.2   USER PARTICIPATION

There are at least three ways in which user participation facilitates organizational implementation (Markus and Mao, 2004): improved system quality, psychological buy-in, and emergent relationships between the users and the implementation team. Improved system quality ensues because the users bring detailed knowledge about their work and how it is concretely done. In contrast, others—such as managers—merely have abstract knowledge about the users' work and often mistake prescriptions of how the work should be done for descriptions of how it is done (Button and Sharrock, 2009). Buy-in ensues because the users become psychologically involved in the change process and committed to the system. For example, Bano et al. (2017, p. 2359) quote a user for saying that "overall you feel satisfied when you feel that your voices are being heard." Without participation, the users experience that they are subjected to the change rather than that they commit to it. Relationships between the users and the implementation team facilitate organizational implementation by opening for richer communication and by making the implementation team empathize with the users and their concerns.

In selecting users for participation, it is important that you select a diverse sample of users. A diverse sample ensures that the implementation activities are informed by a variety of inputs. It also helps ensure that the non-participating users feel represented. Multiple studies contend that the selected users should constitute a representative cross-section of the users (e.g., Kujala and Kauppinen, 2004). Mumford (1983, p. 65) recommends a two-tier structure consisting of a steering committee with senior managers and senior user representatives and a project group with "a representative from each major section and function, each grade, age group and sex." Table 5.1 lists the selection criteria identified by Rasmussen et al. (2011) in a study of user participation in IT projects. These criteria mix a concern for representativeness with other concerns, most notably a concern for selecting users who take an interest in technology and want to contribute to the project. Any one project will assign primacy to some of these criteria and neglect others.

Table 5.1: Criteria for selecting users for participation, based on Rasmussen et al. (2011)	
Criterion	**Level** [*]
1. Knowledge of the work domain	Individual
2. Knowledge about information technology	Individual
3. Ability to empathize with others and understand their needs	Individual
4. Interest in the project and a desire to contribute to it	Individual
5. Ability to pass on knowledge and enthusiasm about the system to other users	Individual
6. Readiness to work with technical issues	Individual
7. Understanding of the negotiated nature of design decisions	Individual
8. Representation of different business units relative to their size or importance	Group
9. Equal representation of all geographic and business areas	Group
10. Including extreme or critical users	Group
11. Random selection of users	Group
12. Including everybody	Group
13. Command of a common language	Group
[*] Individual: Criterion relating to the individual user representative; Group: Criterion relating to the group of user representatives.	

Schneider and Sarker (2006) describe an organizational implementation that involved extensive user participation but was discontinued shortly after vendor selection because the preparation phase failed to converge on a shared path forward. That is, user participation must not only be present, the implementation team must also know how to involve the users in a productive way and how to make competent use of their input. For example, user participation is of limited avail if it merely adds more people to activities that are entrapped in single-loop learning (Section 2.3). It is also of limited avail if users are not involved until after the implementation has more or less been planned. In that case, the users are being informed about the implementation to a much larger extent than granted influence on it. Rather, user participation should be initiated during the management adoption process and continue throughout the three organizational-implementation phases.

You cannot presume that the users agree about the new system and associated organizational changes. The system will affect different user groups in different ways. In addition, users differ in their attitudes to change and technology. Hence, the users will perceive the system differently. The user participation must allow for these differences and create a forum for reaching negotiated agreement. An understanding of the negotiated nature of design decisions is one of the traits to look for when you select users for participation (Table 5.1). If agreement is presumed rather than facilitated, then involving many user groups will likely lead to disagreements that block progress and to disillusionment about the lack of progress (e.g., Janssen et al., 2013). To facilitate the participating users in reaching negotiated agreement and making progress, the implementation team should embrace uncertainty, exercise open communication, and in other ways encourage double-loop learning (Section 2.3).

In the preparation phase, workshops are a widely used means for organizing user participation. The workshops may be about analyzing work practices, specifying system configurations, reviewing new procedures, preparing user training, scheduling go-live activities, or any of the other activities described in this chapter. Specifically, the workshops can specify the effects that are pursued with the system. User participation should be central to effects specification. By formulating the pursued effects, the implementation goals can be communicated clearly and the users, including the non-participating users, get a more solid basis for forming expectations about how the system will affect their work. These expectations may increase their interest in making their voices heard, thereby avoiding that few users take an interest in user participation during the preparations but many users look back at it as insufficient when the implementation has proceeded to go-live. This problem has, for example, been documented by Bano et al. (2017).

5.3   EFFECTS SPECIFICATION

Effects specification is meant to help sustain a focus on the benefits to be realized by implementing a new information system (Hertzum and Simonsen, 2011; Ward and Daniel, 2012). Technical development is not sufficient to realize benefits; they presuppose both technical development and organizational implementation. By avoiding a dissociation between technical and organizational development, effects specification facilitates the mutual adaptation of technology and organization. This mutual adaptation is essential to achieving a good fit between the system and the organization.

Simply put, effects are about the practically realized benefits that are achieved by using a system. This makes effects different from system functionality. While the functionality of a system determines what it can in principle be used to do, the effects describe what is achieved in practice when the organization uses the system. In specifying effects, it is important that you make them concrete and assessable (e.g., by means of before/after measurements, see Section 7.2). The following examples of effects are from the implementation of systems in healthcare organizations.

- All information about medication is recorded in the electronic medication record (Granlien and Hertzum, 2009). The rationale for this effect was to reduce the risk of medication errors by reducing information fragmentation.

- Physicians and nurses in the emergency department spend more of their time with the patients (Hertzum and Simonsen, 2013). The rationale for this effect was to convert cold hands (i.e., time spent away from the patients) into warm hands.

- Shorter preoperative fasting times for patients scheduled for surgery (Simonsen et al., 2020). The rationale for this effect was that it would require improved preoperative coordination, which would benefit the hospital as well as the patients.

The first of these examples involved adjusting the division of labor between physicians and nurses, introducing delegated medication orders, deciding the medications and doses for delegated orders, configuring a delegated-medication list in the electronic medication record, and incorporating these changes in the nurses' daily practices. Relatedly, the second and third examples involved configuring a network of electronic whiteboards and devising procedures for their use. All three examples specify desired changes in the clinicians' work and its direct consequences for the patients. Effects can also be about cost-savings, higher customer satisfaction, lower error rates, increased productivity, or any other benefit the organization pursues by implementing a system.

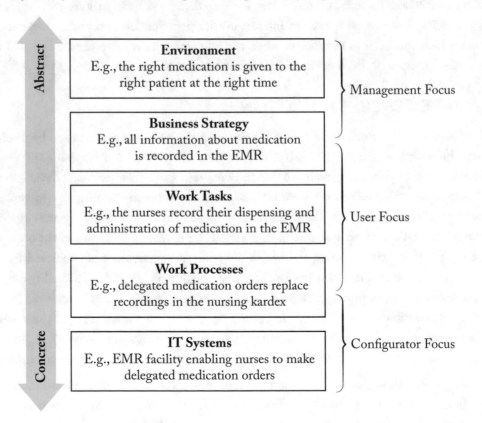

Figure 5.1: Effects hierarchy, based on Hertzum and Simonsen (2011). The example extends an effect for an electronic medication record (EMR) across all five hierarchical levels.

You can think of the effects specified for a system as forming a hierarchy in which higher-level effects give the rationale for lower-level effects (Hertzum and Simonsen, 2011). Analogously, lower-level effects detail how higher-level effects are realized. Figure 5.1 shows an example. Often, higher-level effects are included in business cases to justify new systems. That is, they are specified ahead of organizational implementation. In contrast, the lower-level effects are specified during organizational implementation to make the high-level effects concrete, to provide focus, and to align expectations about the benefits to be realized. The earlier you specify effects, the more they can serve as a unified focus for technical development and organizational implementation.

Figure 5.2 exemplifies the details involved in specifying an effect. When an effect is initially specified, some of the details may not yet be available. The specification is intended as a working document in which empty fields serve as reminders of outstanding issues. At the outset, an effects template with all fields empty can add structure to effects-specification workshops. Simonsen et al. (2011) propose separate effects-specification workshops for management and users because they tend to focus on effects at different levels of abstraction. While management's primary focus is higher-level effects, the users are primarily concerned with effects at the middle and lower levels. This difference reflects that both management and users primarily focus on effects that relate to their tasks and responsibilities. Because their tasks and responsibilities differ, they focus on effects at different levels. It is, however, important to ensure alignment between the higher-level and lower-level effects. The effects hierarchy provides a means for obtaining and representing this alignment.

Effect: Recording medication information in the EMR	Priority: Medium
Description of effect	The nurses record their dispensing and administration of medication in the EMR
Plan for obtaining effect	• Introduction of delegated medication orders to allow nurses to order selected medication • Information and training (during the nurses' morning break) to inform the nurses about the delegated medication orders • One-page pocket guide describing how to perform delegated medication orders in the EMR
Follow-up	Record audits (monthly, for half a year) to establish the number of violations to the requirement that all medication information is recorded in the EMR
Current status	Six violations (at second audit) The target level is zero violations for delegated medication
Barriers	Many activities compete for the nurses' attention. User interface for making delegated medication orders in the EMR is somewhat unintuitive
Stakeholders	Registered nurses, excluding temps

Figure 5.2: Example of the specification of an effect for an electronic medication record (EMR), based on Granlien and Hertzum (2009).

The specification of effects clarifies the planned change and provides a basis for following up on whether it is realized after go-live. However, organizational implementation cannot be planned ahead in its entirety. To avoid overemphasizing the planned change, two reservations are in order. First, it may prove impossible to freeze the process of continuous organizational change long enough for the organizational implementation to rebalance the direction of change (Section 2.2). In other words, there is a risk that effects specified early in a long preparation phase are rendered irrelevant by the continuous changes that happen between specification and go-live. You should not pursue irrelevant effects, but it can be difficult to agree on whether an effect has become irrelevant. Second, the operational use of the system after go-live will reveal unplanned, positive opportunities and unforeseen, negative side effects. To capitalize on the opportunities, they must be acknowledged as new effects on par with the planned effects. To avoid the side effects, you may have to revise or abandon some of the planned effects.

5.4   USER TRAINING, SYSTEM CONFIGURATION, TASK PROCEDURES, AND INCENTIVES

You prepare an organization for go-live by making its people, technology, tasks, and structure ready for the use of the new information system (Figure 2.1). Effects specification sets the course and helps sustain the focus of these preparations. On that basis, the users are trained, the technology is configured, the tasks are redefined by new procedures, and the structure is revised by aligning incentives with the new ways of working. It complicates the preparations that these activities are interdependent.

User training aims to provide users with the knowledge and skills they need in performing their tasks with the new system. Training improves the perceived ease of use and perceived usefulness of the system and, thereby, increases adoption (Figure 3.3). Many studies have documented the positive effect of user training on organizational implementation (Gupta et al., 2010; Sabherwal et al., 2006; Sharma and Yetton, 2007). To make training effective, you must combine instruction for knowledge and overview with hands-on experiences for practical skills and appreciation of details. When conducted by gathering an instructor and a group of users, there are opportunities for asking questions and for discussion among the users about how to handle frequent and special cases. These opportunities must be furnished in other ways if training consists of e-learning material that users process individually.

For large organizational implementations, user training typically follows a train-the-trainers approach (Pearce et al., 2012) in which a small group of super users receives in-depth training and then trains everyone else. If training is too early, then the new system, procedures, or incentives will not be finalized for the training sessions. In addition, the users may forget what they learn if they do not need it in their work shortly after training (Norton et al., 2012). If training is too late, then uncertainty builds about what it will be like to work with the system and some users will not receive training until after go-live. Late training also precludes that usability problems identified during training can be fixed before go-live. The need for training is negligible if, and only if, the system is straightforward, it is not accompanied by strategic change, and the users are willing to learn to use it while they use it.

System configuration aims to adapt the system to the organization. Depending on the system and organization, configurations can range from small changes to large extensions. Large extensions are normally made by the system vendor's technical developers. Smaller changes can be made by technical developers or by the implementation team. Irrespective of their size, configurations must be tightly linked to decisions about how to adapt the organization to the system. Large-scale suite systems such as ERP systems and electronic health records are extensively configurable. Other systems provide fewer configuration possibilities. The types of configurations that are possible with the system and relevant for the organization can take multiple forms (Brehm et al., 2001; Uppström et al., 2015).

- *Parameter settings:* choosing between different executions of system functions.

- *Data conversion:* configuring data for import, presentation, or export.

- *Screen masks:* creating screens for the entry or presentation of information by using screen-formatting options in the system.

- *Report generation:* setting up extended data export and reporting options in a report generator integrated in the system.

- *Script programming:* creating functionality or workflow support by means of macros or a script language integrated in the system.

- *API programming:* creating functionality by using an application programming interface (API).

- *Add-ons:* installing third-party packages designed to extend the system with specific functionality.

- *Interface development:* programming interfaces to legacy systems and third-party products.

- *Source-code modification:* finalizing or changing the source code of the system.

You can make configurations at different levels. Some configurations cover all uses of the system and enforce organization-level workflows and standards. These configurations require discussions and decisions that cut across business units. Other configurations are specific to business units and may, for example, introduce department-specific functionality or setups. These configurations may be made by intra-departmental super users. Still other configuration possibilities may allow individual users to customize the system for their personal needs and preferences. These configuration possibilities become relevant after go-live. Longhurst et al. (2019) find that users who utilize the configuration possibilities to customize their system for their personal needs are substantially more satisfied with it than users who do not customize their system. In contrast, Haines (2009) advocates a mindful approach to configuration to avoid customizations that are costly to make but add little value.

New procedures adapt the organization to the system by redefining how tasks are performed. Devising new procedures requires a solid understanding of how work is accomplished in the organization (Ellingsen et al., 2007). Therefore, users from the business units affected by the system should participate as subject matter experts. In addition, new procedures cannot be devised without a solid understanding of the possibilities afforded by the new system. To provide this understanding, some of the people involved in configuring the system must also participate in devising the new procedures. Finally, management may participate—directly or by stipulating the terms of reference for the work with devising new procedures. Management will want to ensure compliance with strategic intents.

Bureaucratic organizations (Section 2.4) have standard operating procedures for many tasks and formal structures for revising and communicating these procedures. Organic organizations have established practices but are unlikely to have procedures that formally describe them. Thus, organic organizations have less support in place for helping you prepare new ways of working. These organizations rely somewhat less on preparations and correspondingly more on devising new practices after go-live as part of system use. Furthermore, the complexity of devising new procedures varies with task type. Because value-chain tasks (e.g., production and distribution) tend to be more interdependent than business-support tasks (e.g., accounting and human resources), it takes longer to devise new procedures for value-chain tasks (Santamaría-Sánchez et al., 2010).

Incentives are extrinsic motivators that aim to make it appealing for the individual users to adopt the system. In addition, users may be intrinsically motivated by the specified effects that state how the users' work will benefit from the system. Often, the incentive structure rewards individual accomplishments, whereas the system requires—and seeks to foster and streamline—collaboration. Such misalignment threatens adoption by requiring that users forgo the pursuit of rewards and recognition to make effective use of the system (Olson and Olson, 2014; Orlikowski, 2000). Unless the incentive structure is brought into alignment with the intended ways of working, the system will likely remain underused. To accomplish such alignment, the implementation team must work closely with management. Incentives are also important because a system may be beneficial to the organization but unappealing to some staff groups, who experience higher workload, eroded influence, increased monotony, loss of specialist knowledge, or otherwise less attractive jobs. To make these users embrace the system, they must be compensated.

As an example, Markus and Keil (1994, p. 13) analyze the organizational implementation of a system that remained largely unused by the sales reps it was designed to support, for two reasons. First, "sales reps were not motivated to do what the system enabled them to do"—the absence of a substantial booster. Second, "using the system made it harder for them to do what they were motivated to do"—the presence of a substantial barrier. These two disincentives remained unrecognized, or at least unaddressed, while the organization spent years of effort and millions of dollars on implementation activities. Misaligned incentives are often difficult to address for the implementation team. The incentive structures available to you in realigning incentives are dictated by management, thereby limiting your options. Furthermore, symbolic incentives, such as what counts as prestigious, may be determined outside the organization, for example by the norms within a profession (Andersen, 2009). Thus, management is also limited in its options because it is only in control of a subset of the incentives that influence the adoption decisions of the staff.

5.5   PILOT IMPLEMENTATION

The preparation phase takes place in a sort of vacuum created by the absence of feedback. It is not until the users start using the system at go-live that it will become apparent whether the user training, system configurations, and other preparations are sufficient. To obtain feedback earlier, the implementation team has the possibility of staging use activities before go-live. Pilot implementations serve this purpose (Hertzum et al., 2012). They create design-in-use opportunities prior to go-live. The purpose of pilot implementations is threefold:

- *To obtain feedback from real use before go-live:* In contrast to usability testing, which is done in lab-like settings during technical development, pilot implementation involves subjecting the system to all the complications and vagaries of real use (Hertzum, 2018).

- *To inform the finalization of technical and organizational development:* Pilot implementations must be completed sufficiently early to allow time for adjusting the system and organizational preparations before go-live, but they cannot be performed until the system has been properly engineered (Hertzum et al., 2012).

- *To test whether to continue or discontinue the organizational implementation:* Pilot implementations are tests; they are not to be confused with incremental implementation (Section 6.1). They provide a decision point for de-escalating troubled projects by abandoning them (Montealegre and Keil, 2000).

A pilot implementation involves many of the same activities as a full organizational implementation but at a smaller scale; see Figure 5.3. During *planning and design*, the pilot site is selected.

A fairly self-contained site is preferable because it reduces the need for extra support to handle the interactions between the site, which uses the pilot system, and the rest of the organization, which does not. However, a self-contained site may not exist. The planning-and-design activity also involves determining how the lessons learned during the pilot implementation will be collected.

During *technical configuration*, the pilot system is configured for the pilot site. This activity includes migrating production data to the pilot system and setting up interfaces to other systems at the pilot site. It can also involve setting up simulations of interfaces. Hertzum et al. (2012) describe a case in which system interactions with organizational units external to the pilot site were simulated by a back office staffed around the clock. The back-office staff continuously monitored the pilot system for such interactions, mailed them in the conventional paper-based fashion, waited for the results to arrive back, and immediately typed them into the pilot system. Thus, the pilot users experienced the system as if all transactions were fully IT supported.

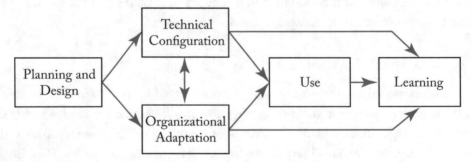

Figure 5.3: The five activities in a pilot implementation, based on Hertzum et al. (2012).

During *organizational adaptation*, the pilot site revises its procedures to benefit from the pilot system. Like for organizational implementation in general, this activity is particularly complex when the system spans multiple, partly autonomous organizations. Many communication and coordination systems fall in this category. For such systems, the organizational adaptations involve reaching a negotiated agreement among stakeholders who are not under a common management. If the use domain is politically textured, these negotiations can be knotty and lengthy (Mønsted et al., 2020). The pilot site must also set up safeguards against user errors and system breakdowns, which are more likely with a pilot system than a finalized system.

During *use*, real work is performed with the pilot system. This activity involves striking a balance between incorporating the system in the work at the pilot site and maintaining a focus on the system as an object under evaluation. The period of pilot use should ideally be long enough for practices to stabilize because that provides the most robust basis for learning from the pilot implementation. However, the resources consumed by pilot implementations, such as staffing a back office around the clock, often limit their duration. In practice, the period of pilot use can range from a few days (e.g., Pal et al., 2008) to several months (e.g., Mønsted et al., 2020).

The final pilot-implementation activity, *learning*, is the objective of pilot implementations. It involves the collection of information about the introduction and use of the system at the pilot site. You learn from the period of pilot use as well as from the preceding pilot-implementation activities. In learning from a pilot implementation, it is important to focus on those of its aspects that reflect what it will be like to implement and use the system in the entire organization. However, these aspects may be difficult to distinguish from the aspects that are specific to the pilot implementation, such as aspects brought about by simulating some system functionality. Hertzum et al. (2019) find that many difficulties in learning from pilot implementations involve expectations about a clear division between these two kinds of aspects but difficulties in telling them apart in practice.

Pilot implementation complements usability testing, it is not an alternative to usability testing. Usability tests are normally conducted in lab-like settings away from real work to test a system prototype that is not yet ready for use in operational settings (Hertzum, 2020). In contrast, pilot implementations are conducted in real-life settings to test a pilot system that is properly engineered but not yet finalized. While a usability test is directed at the fit between user and system, a pilot implementation is directed at the fit between organization and system. Because the pilot system is used for real work, the objective of learning about the fit between organization and system is added to the objectives that come with performing the real work. As a consequence, the learning objective may be considered secondary to other objectives, such as getting the daily work done. The implementation team must work to ensure that the pilot users are, and remain, committed to the pilot implementation and its learning objective. Unless the learning objective is carefully managed, it is likely to suffer (Hertzum et al., 2012). If you manage it carefully, a pilot implementation is a convincing and effective preparation activity.

5.6   CHAMPIONS

During the preparation phase, organizations have expectations toward their new system to a much larger extent than they have experiences with it. The predominance of expectations is especially large for the majority of the users who do not participate in pilot implementations or other preparations. An important part of preparing the organization for the system is to build positive expectations and create buy-in. To succeed in this, the preparations cannot be completed within the implementation team; it is essential that the users at large build positive expectations and buy in to the system. Champions are key to these outreach efforts by serving as advocates for the system in their network of organizational contacts (Thakhathi, 2018).

Champions are persons who throw their weight behind a system and thereby boost its adoption in an organization (Beath, 1991; Rogers, 2003). If the champion is a manager, then the manager's formal position in the organization contributes to the influence that the champion will be able to exert on others' adoption of the system. The need for a champion with managerial power increases with the cost and radicalness of the system. However, champions can also be users with an informal position that lets them influence their colleagues' adoption of the system. Champions who are users tend to be perceived as more credible by other users. Whether a manager or a user, a champion is so important in overcoming indifference and creating goodwill toward a new system that Schön (1963, p. 84) states: "The new idea either finds a champion or dies." It is in this sense that champions are your key collaborators in the preparation phase. Obviously, they are not the only collaborator of importance.

By championing a system, people put themselves on the line for a system that has yet to prove its value to the organization. To be prepared to do so, champions must be innovation-minded and willing to take risks. If the system fails, its champion will be associated with the failure and possibly blamed for misleading the organization by persuading it to adopt a system that is unappealing in retrospect. In addition, champions' innovation-mindedness is often accompanied by a preparedness for double-loop learning—for being open to questioning assumptions and reformulating goals. This preparedness tends to be uncommon, especially in bureaucratic organizations. The risk associated with championing a system may discourage people from assuming the role. The incentive structure should recognize this risk and reward the people who voluntarily champion a new system. Otherwise, organizational implementations are left with the option of an appointed champion.

In appointing a champion, the qualities you should look for are network, charisma, and people skills. Rogers (2003) elaborates these qualities by stating that champions must (1) occupy a linking position in their organization, (2) possess analytic and intuitive skills in understanding diverse persons' aspirations, and (3) demonstrate interpersonal and negotiation skills in working with other people. These qualities make champions likely go-to persons when people in the organization need information or advice, thereby creating many opportunities for the champions to facilitate the approval and adoption of the new system. As go-to persons, the champions get to tailor their messages about the system to people's specific concerns and to do so when people are open to input (Norton et al., 2012). Being charismatic, the champions also have the ability to inspire others with their enthusiasm.

CHAPTER 6

Going Live: The Initial, Planned Change

Up until go-live, the implementation activities are performed by a dedicated implementation team away from the primary work of the organization. From go-live onward, implementation success is dependent on how all the users in the organization incorporate the system in their work. This shift is challenging for several reasons. Time-honored practices must be discontinued, thereby creating uncertainty about how to accomplish tasks. The new system and procedures must be taken into use, thereby increasing workload and the risk of mistakes. Defects and inconveniences will be encountered in the system and procedures, thereby requiring temporary precautions and ad hoc action. The primary work is disrupted, thereby necessitating patience and a positive attitude in a stressful situation. To succeed, the planned change must be well prepared and it must be insisted upon in the face of immediate difficulties and disturbances.

Any organizational implementation involves deciding whether the implementation strategy should be big bang or incremental. This chapter starts by discussing this decision (Section 6.1). Irrespective of the implementation strategy, go-live involves migrating data from the old to the new system (Section 6.2) and taking precautions to safeguard against errors (Section 6.3). These precautions include having support staff on site during go-live. In spite of the precautions, the most common immediate consequence of go-live is a dip in productivity (Section 6.4). It is not until productivity returns to baseline that the organization starts reaping benefit from the new system. However, the return to baseline productivity can be upset by problems, including problems that should have been solved during the preparations but were overlooked or underestimated. Such exported problems (Section 6.5) will emerge during go-live because it subjects the planned change to all the particulars involved in actually performing the primary work. Your key collaborators during go-live are the super users, who are tasked with easing the users into their new ways of working (Section 6.6).

6.1 BIG BANG OR INCREMENTAL IMPLEMENTATION?

Go-live is disruptive because it introduces changes. It can be approached as a shock that should be absorbed as quickly as possible or as gently as possible. These two approaches lead to opposing implementation strategies: big bang and incremental implementation. The strengths of the big-bang strategy tend to be the weaknesses of incremental implementation, and vice versa; see Table 6.1.

Table 6.1: Big bang vs. incremental implementation

	Big Bang	Incremental Implementation
Definition	All-at-once switch from old to new system and procedures	Gradual switch from old to new system and procedures
Scope	Large; can be difficult to manage	Small increments; easier to manage
Timeframe	Short; aims to move quickly to benefits capture	Long; prioritizes low risk over quick move to benefits capture
Momentum	Maintains momentum	May run out of steam
Risk	High; if it fails, it fails spectacularly	Low; if something goes wrong, it can be remedied before the next increment
Anxiety	High, but short-lived	Low, but for an extended period of time
Resources	Many resources must be allocated, but for a short period of time	Requires fewer resources and they can move from one increment to the next

Big bang involves that all users start using all parts of the new system at once. That is, there is one go-live date. Up until this date, the old system and procedures are in use throughout the organization. From the next day, the new system and procedures are in use throughout the organization. Big bang is a high-risk, high-reward strategy (Brown and Vessey, 2001; Owens, 2008). If something goes wrong in one business unit, then it can have a domino effect that impacts the entire organizational implementation. In addition, many resources must be allocated to go-live because the implementation team must be sufficiently large to support all users simultaneously. And just as the users have no experience with using the system for real work, the implementation team has no experience with the issues that will emerge when the system is put to operational use. To handle the risk associated with big bang, some organizations temporarily shut down production when extensive systems go live. For example, a high-tech manufacturer took the drastic step of shutting down production for ten days to migrate all data to its new system, perform final tests, and go live with the new system and procedures (McAfee, 2002). Other organizations, such as news media, do not have the option of temporarily shutting down; they need to handle go-live in parallel with their primary work.

The main attraction of big bang is that it keeps go-live brief. Thus, the anxiety associated with go-live should be short-lived, the disturbance of the primary work should be temporary, and the progression to benefits capture should be quick. Keeping go-live brief also makes it easier for the implementation team to maintain momentum. Tyre and Orlikowski (1994) find that the window of opportunity for changing procedures after starting to use a new system is brief; the change process quickly loses momentum because most users prioritize attending to their primary work over exploring the new system. A further argument for switching quickly from the old to the new system is problems with the old system. Brown and Vessey (2001) describe a case in which the IT support staff spent most of their time resolving disconnects among the legacy systems. The new system responded to an urgent need for freeing their time for other, more strategic tasks. Relatedly, Sarkis and Sundaray (2003) describe a case in which an organization needed up to 6 months to deliver products that their best competitors could deliver in less than 30 days. The new system helped respond to an urgent need for faster product delivery.

In contrast to big bang, *incremental implementation* involves that the implementation of the new system is divided into increments that are spread over a period of time. That is, go-live consists of a series of go-live dates, one for each increment (Leon, 2019; Owens, 2008). Figure 6.1 illustrates the process, which is well-suited for agile projects (Bider and Jalali, 2016). If the increments are system modules, then the result is module-by-module implementation. The increments can also be organizational sites. If so, the result is site-by-site implementation. Further variants of incremental implementation include case-by-case implementation in which the characteristics of the individual work case determines when it is moved from the old to the new system. With all variants, the rationale is to reduce risk and obtain a more even pull on implementation-team resources. The lower risk is obtained by the increments, which restrict the consequences of problems to the increment and allows for learning from one increment to the next. By allowing for learning, the incremental approach to implementation reduces anxiety and causes smaller peaks in cognitive load (Culp et al., 2005). In addition, the implementation team learns from one increment to the next and becomes an important conduit for disseminating early experiences with the system when they move from one business unit to another.

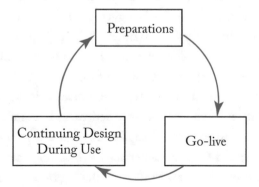

Figure 6.1: Incremental implementation consists of dividing the implementation of a system into increments that are implemented one at a time, thereby creating an iterative process.

The downside of incremental implementation is that it prolongs the period during which the organization is transitioning from the old to the new system. As a consequence, it takes longer before the organization reaps the full benefit of the new system and there is a risk that the implementation process runs out of steam before it reaches completion. Brown and Vessey (2001) find that this risk is a major argument for managers to choose against incremental implementation. In addition, incremental implementation cannot do away with risk and anxiety, only reduce them. For large systems, Ross (1999, p. 67) contends that "even with careful planning and training, going live usually is highly disruptive." Thus, users may not experience an appreciable reduction in risk and anxiety. They may primarily experience incremental implementation as a prolonged state of risk, anxiety, and increased workload.

Owens (2008) recommends restricting big bang to small organizations because their limited size ensures that the scope of the implementation is contained. The limited size also increases the likelihood that you have all users on board. For similar reasons, large organizations can choose the big-bang strategy for small, or uncritical, systems. When implementing large systems in large organizations, an incremental strategy is recommended. Even a series of go-lives in fairly quick succession provides valuable possibilities for learning, fixing problems, and reducing risk (Sarkis and Sundaray, 2003).

6.2   DATA MIGRATION

Whether the implementation strategy is big bang or incremental implementation, the data in the old system must be migrated to the new system. Depending on the system, these data may be more or less dynamic and more or less extensive. Normally, they are essential to the organization because they enable its effective and efficient operation. For example: (1) new orders are recorded to notify production and ensure timely delivery; (2) production data are logged for reference purposes and to provide traceability; (3) the use of supplies is logged to know when stocks must be replenished; (4) task assignments are registered to inform staff and balance workload; (5) case assessments are written to explain actions and enable follow-up; (6) data series are recorded for quality assessment and product improvement; (7) changes are registered to keep track of how plans evolve and what status is; (8) meetings are documented in minutes to summarize decisions and arguments; (9) policies and procedures are written down to improve practices and ensure compliance; (10) payments are registered to keep track of expenses; (11) staff performance is recorded to determine training needs and calculate bonuses; and (12) customer feedback is documented to spot problems and enable data mining. Without timely access to its data, the organization grinds to a halt. Thus, data migration needs to be smooth.

The benefits of new systems often include that they reduce data fragmentation by merging several old systems into one unified system. As a result, the data must not just be moved, they must also be connected in new ways. These new connections must be established on the basis of the data available in the old, disconnected systems. As an example, Hertzum (2002) describes the implementation of a system for handling child support and alimony (CSA) cases in Danish municipalities. Because the person obliged to pay CSA and the person entitled to receive CSA payment normally live in different municipalities, the old system had separate CSA cases for the payer and payee. The payer's CSA case was handled by the municipality in which the payer lived and the payee's CSA case by the municipality in which the payee lived. However, the new CSA system combined the two cases into one unified case to enable new facilities and remove shortcomings.

Establishing this seemingly simple connection turned out to be a complex matter, even though every Danish citizen has a unique social security number. Like other municipal systems, the CSA system used the social security number for identifying people. However, people who are Danish residents but not Danish citizens have a surrogate social security number rather than a genuine one. For some reason, surrogate social security numbers were assigned by the individual municipality without any coordination of the numbers assigned by different municipalities. Thus, persons in different municipalities could have the same surrogate number. This was not a problem in the old system because all its transactions were intra-municipal, but it created considerable problems in migrating the data to the new system, which combined data across municipal borders. In addition, a person could be the payer in several CSA cases. The old system allowed for collapsing these several cases into one case. During the data migration such collapsed cases, which were not uncommon, had to be split into independent cases before they were paired with the cases for the payees. For these collapsed cases, the problem was not so much identifying the right persons as correctly dividing the payments among the payee cases.

Data migration must be carefully prepared but cannot happen until go-live because the old system produces and updates data right until it is taken out of operation. At the same time, data migration should be completed at go-live because the new system is not fully operational until all data have been transferred. However, data migration is not instantaneous. For a period after go-live, it is often necessary to look up some data in the old system because they are not yet available in the new system. Their correct conversion and transfer may, for example, involve manual processing (Culp et al., 2005). Similarly, some facilities in the new system may not be operational or accurate because they depend on data that have not yet been transferred. With a big-bang strategy, every effort is made to shorten this transition period. It is easier for the users to tolerate inconvenient access and missing functionality if it is for a brief period only.

With incremental implementation, a longer transition period is accepted to reduce risk but at the cost of prolonging the inconveniences and functionality reductions. For example, in the site-by-site implementation of a new sales system, neither the old system nor the new can provide organization-wide sales information during the transition period. Without this information, stocks may not be replenished in time, deliveries may be delayed, and customers may not return. If organization-wide sales information is pertinent, then data from the sites that have started using the new system must be copied to the old system for the generation of correct organization-wide sales information. Such copying adds costs and introduces additional possibilities for error.

6.3   PRECAUTIONS AGAINST ERRORS

Careful preparations are no guarantee against difficulties and errors during go-live. On the contrary, it is well-known that information systems have unintended side effects in addition to the planned effects covered by the preparations (e.g., Nworie and Haughton, 2008; Parks et al., 2017; Sergeeva et al., 2016). In the short run, starting to use a system will likely reveal some ill-chosen system configurations, incomplete procedures, erroneously converted data, dysfunctional system integrations, and difficult-to-use facilities. There will be many opportunities for mistakes, oversights, and other troubles. The users are understandably uncertain about how the system will influence their work and may be anxious about the extra workload during go-live. For these reasons, go-live entails insisting on the planned change in the face of immediate disturbances. This requires that the implementation team sets up precautions to safeguard go-live against errors. Common precautions include less work, extra staff, on-site support, extra training sessions, status meetings, and running the old system in parallel with the new.

Less work: With planning, it is usually possible to reduce the amount of primary work that needs to be completed during go-live. Reducing the amount of primary work makes time for the users to get acquainted with how the new system and procedures function in practice. Scheduled activities can be kept to a minimum during go-live, thereby reducing the workload to the ad hoc activities. Non-critical activities can be rescheduled or cancelled altogether. For example, a hospital can reschedule elective surgeries but must continue to perform acute surgeries. In addition, you can schedule go-live outside the periods that are known to be most busy. For this reason, many systems go live during a weekend.

Extra staff: If it is not possible to reduce the amount of work, then extra staff can be called in. With more hands for performing the work, each user has less work to complete. The extra hands can be regular staff who are requested to work overtime or they can be temps who are hired specifically for go-live. In site-by-site implementations, you may consider calling in staff from other sites. If these sites have already gone live, then their staff will bring valuable experience with the new ways of working. If not, their staff will gain valuable experience for the upcoming go-live at their own site. In addition, external consultants from the preparation phase sometimes have sufficient domain knowledge to step in as extra hands during go-live. However, they more often serve as on-site support.

On-site support: During go-live, the users will frequently need support. To ensure quick and easy access to support, it should be available on site during the first and most hectic days. By having support staff on site, they can both provide support when requested and offer support when they find that it is needed. This way, the support staff also serves to spot impending errors and oversights, thereby preventing them before they cause harm. After the first hectic days or weeks, you can reduce the support to an on-call service or hotline. At this stage, the support staff may be heading on to go-live at the next site. The support staff is usually super users (Section 6.6) but can also be consultants from the preparation phase.

Extra training sessions: Some users, such as temps, may not have received user training before go-live. In addition, on-site support may involve repeating the same information many times to different users. To reiterate key information and disseminate new information, extra training sessions should be conducted. These sessions should address issues that have emerged during the on-site support and could not be resolved on the spot. They may also involve exchanges among the attending users about how to make effective use of the system. To improve attendance in spite of the busyness following go-live, Owens (2008) suggests that you organize the extra training as fairly informal lunch-and-learn sessions.

Status meetings and system-output checks: The implementation team should meet with site representatives (e.g., its management and super users) shortly before go-live to verify that the site is ready. One item on the agenda for this meeting is to identify a local person to whom the implementation team can escalate issues that it is unable to resolve. Culp et al. (2005) find that this person is rarely activated, but invaluable when needed. For a period after go-live, the implementation team and the site representatives should meet daily or weekly to discuss status and follow up on any outstanding issues. As input to these meetings, Brown and Vessey (2001) recommend instituting a process for checking the system output in areas where problems are likely to first be visible. Doing these checks daily for the first week or month provides assurance that the system functions properly—or early warnings if it does not.

Running the old system in parallel: For systems that are critical to business, safety, or society, it may be warranted to keep the old system running in parallel with the new system for some time. This way, the organization can revert to the old system at any point, should the new system fail. However, running two systems in parallel doubles the work and delays the return on investment. When it is deemed necessary, temps are normally brought in to run the old system, while the regular staff uses the new system. In addition to providing a fallback in case of failure, the parallel output from the old system provides a first-rate basis for checking the correctness of the output from the new system. Running the old system in parallel is intended to allow time for the organization to build confidence in the new system but it may, unintentionally, give the impression that the organization is not fully committed to the new system. It is for the implementation team, supported by management and champions, to avoid this misinterpretation through their communication activities.

6.4   PRODUCTIVITY DIP

Go-live consumes attention and other resources. As a result, fewer resources are available for the primary work, which suffers a temporary setback. This setback takes the form of a productivity dip; see Figure 6.2. Normally, productivity starts to decrease shortly before go-live because many resources are consumed by the final preparations, such as user training (McAfee, 2002). The main dip co-occurs with go-live (Ross, 1999). A direct contributor to the productivity dip is the precaution of rescheduling work to reduce the amount of work that needs to be completed during go-live. Sometimes, this rescheduling amounts to a complete shutdown of production for a brief period, especially during big bangs. However, the main reason for the productivity dip is that users have to reshuffle their activities to accommodate the slowdown caused by lacking established practices for how to get their work done.

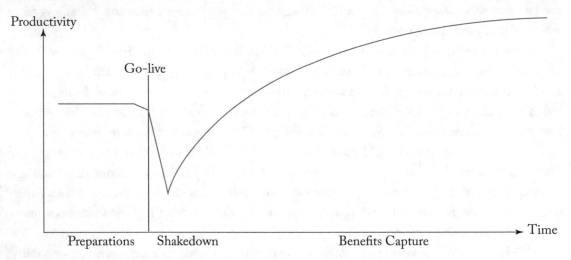

Figure 6.2: Productivity dip that accompanies go-live, based on Ross (1999) and McAfee (2002).

The return to baseline production is a learning process and follows a learning curve that hopefully continues beyond baseline to yield productivity gains (Figure 6.2). The characteristic shape of a learning curve indicates that early efforts yield near immediate returns but also that later efforts yield diminishing returns (Gattiker and Goodhue, 2005; McAfee, 2002). Clearly, the go-live date is not the end of the organizational implementation, but the starting point of the manifold activities involved in troubleshooting, reaching the state of routine use, and deriving benefit from the system. Initially, the users experience substantial disruptions to established practices and find themselves suffering from difficult adjustments to new circumstances, combined with incomplete data and occasional system malfunctions. These difficulties, incompletenesses, and malfunctions occur in spite of a thorough preparation phase. They surface at go-live because it subjects the system to the full complexity of how work is accomplished in the organization. A pilot implementation (Section 5.5) is the only way in which you can prepare the organization for the unanticipated aspects of this complexity.

Over time, the users become familiar with the new system and establish work routines that blend the new procedures with local extensions and workarounds. This process proceeds faster and further if the implementation team handles problems swiftly and with due consideration for local particulars. To do so, the implementation team must interact frequently with users to learn about the problems and it must have the executive power to task developers, configurators, super users, and others with fixing the problems. The importance of reacting swiftly to problems is emphasized by Saeed et al. (2010), who find that five months after go-live the use of a new system is inversely related to task efficiency. That is, the more the system is adopted and used, the larger the productivity dip. To avoid that this inverse relationship persists, problems must be ironed out as quickly as possible.

While the productivity dip is a very real phenomenon, the graph of the productivity dip (Figure 6.2) serves illustrative purposes only. Three provisos are warranted. First, the depth of the productivity dip varies with the organization, system, and implementation process. Some 25% of organizations even appear to avoid a productivity dip altogether (Saeed et al., 2010). For obvious reasons, a small dip is preferable to a large one. However, in industries with narrow profit margins even a small productivity dip may be serious (Arvidsson et al., 2014). In addition, organizations that provide public services are under an obligation to uphold these services. Thus, the mere prospect of a productivity dip can be a barrier that makes people reluctant to adopt a new system (McGinn et al., 2011).

Second, the duration of the productivity dip also varies. For extensive, organization-wide systems, organizations should expect a productivity dip that lasts about 3 months (McAfee, 2002), 3–9 months (Ali and Miller, 2017), or 4–12 months (Ross, 1999). It will be even longer before gains in productivity start to appear; estimates for example suggest more than 18 months (Tam et al., 2019) and 1–2 years (Saeed et al., 2010). By distinguishing between productivity gains at the individual and organizational level, Jurison (1996) finds that gains in the productivity of individual staff can be reliably measured 6–8 months after go-live whereas gains in organizational productivity mainly start in the second year after go-live.

Third, productivity with the new system may never increase beyond the baseline level. The clearest evidence for this disturbing point is the large number of failed and troubled organizational implementations. The possible reasons are many (see Chapter 3), including partial adoption. With partial adoption, the local improvements obtained with a system dissipate in the downstream process before they result in organizational productivity gains. As an example of a successful organizational implementation, Sedera and Lokuge (2020) find 11%, 13%, and 3% performance improvements for operational, managerial, and executive users, respectively, in the period from 6 months to 6 years after an ERP system went live.

To illustrate the possible impact of these three provisos on the productivity dip, Figure 6.3 shows four variants of how productivity may evolve after go-live. The four variants include no productivity gain, system rejection, no productivity dip, and a productivity gain achieved through a series of distinct efforts and learning processes. The last of these variants emphasizes how benefits capture is accomplished by continuing design during use (see Chapter 7).

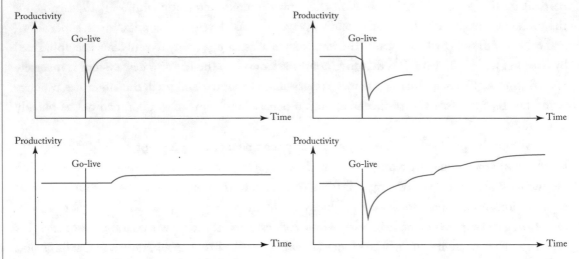

Figure 6.3: Variants of the productivity dip following go-live—brief productivity dip but no benefit beyond baseline (top left), system rejection after prolonged productivity dip (top right), no productivity dip but only slight benefit (bottom left), and productivity dip followed by return to baseline, improvement beyond baseline achieved through continuing design in use (bottom right).

6.5   EXPORTED PROBLEMS

Go-live is the phase in which many problems are recognized because users start to experience their consequences (Wagner and Piccoli, 2007). Some of the problems are the result of errors and oversights that have remained dormant since they were made in the preparation phase or during technical development. Similarly, some of the errors and oversights that are made during go-live may remain unrealized until it later turns out that they prevent benefits capture. Markus (2004) terms such problems exported problems because they are not fixed in the phase in which they originate but rather passed on to later phases. When exported problems show up, it may be too late or too expensive to fix them.

Table 6.2 gives examples of problems that are commonly exported from technical development to organizational implementation, from its preparation phase to later phases, and from go-live to benefits capture. Several of the problems are about paying insufficient attention to benefits realization by underspecifying the planned change. These problems include a vague business case, not using it after it has been approved, and failing to specify the pursued effects (Einhorn et al., 2019; Hertzum and Simonsen, 2011; Markus, 2004). Without clarity about the pursued effects, it is impossible for the implementation team to follow up on whether they are realized. Thereby, it remains unknown whether additional implementation activities are needed.

Table 6.2: Exported problems in the organizational implementation of information systems	
Phase	**Problems Commonly Exported**
Technical development	• Inadequate analysis or business case, thereby leaving it underspecified how the system will be of benefit to the organization • Scope cuts that reduce or postpone system functionality, thereby weakening the fit between the system and the users' tasks • Shortcuts in system testing, thereby leaving the organization without solid knowledge about system defects • Continuing technical development right up until go-live, thereby not providing a stable basis for system testing and user training • An insufficiently configurable system, thereby making it difficult for the implementation team to adapt the system to the organization
Preparations	• Failing to recognize that the implementation of an information system involves organizational change and requires change management • Failing to specify the effects pursued with the implementation of the system and associated procedures • Mismatch between the pursued effects and the incentive structure in place to motivate the users • Inadequate communication about the need for the new system and procedures as well as about its constraints • User training is too early, too little, or too late, thereby leaving users unready for performing their work with the new system • Underestimating the need for precautions against errors, thereby increasing the likelihood of stress and errors • Underestimating the productivity dip, thereby creating frustration, dissatisfaction, and unmet budgets when it continues unexpectedly
Go-live	• Ceasing to explore new ways of working as soon as a way forward has been found, thereby adopting suboptimal practices • Failing to abandon workarounds adopted to cope with early problems that have later been fixed • Failure to converge on new collaborative practices, thereby creating a prolonged need for additional ad hoc coordination • Few users are sufficiently technology savvy and knowledgeable about the system to be ready to start tinkering with it

Other exported problems are about underestimating the time and resources needed for activities such as system testing, user training, precautions against errors, and for recovering from the productivity dip. With insufficient time and resources for these activities, the users feel unprepared, overwhelmed, and frustrated when they, at go-live, experience a longer-than-expected increase in problems and workload combined with a decrease in performance (Häkkinen and Hilmola, 2008). This experience of unmet expectations may lead to partial adoption and, for some users, even to system rejection. In their turn, partial adoption and full rejection increase the need for you to follow up on benefits realization.

The problems exported from go-live to the benefits-capture phase concern the users' reactions to the system, procedures, and experienced difficulties. If the users are eager to get on with their daily work, they will tend to accept the first functional solution they come across when they are blocked in their work (Reijonen and Heikkilä, 2006; Tyre and Orlikowski, 1994). As long as this solution works, they will neither question it, nor seek alternative options. Thus, suboptimal practices may ensue. If a workaround is adopted to solve a temporary problem, the users may not abandon the workaround when you have later fixed the problem, either because they are not aware that it has been fixed or because they see no need to abandon a functional way of working. While functional, this way of working may water down the planned effects of implementing the system.

Problems end up exported for several reasons. First, exporting a problem frees resources for attending to problems that cannot be exported. In a resource-constrained, deadline-driven organizational implementation, it may be effective—in the short run—to export problems. However, exported problems emerge at some point. For many problems, this point is go-live.

Second, a problem that cannot be satisfactorily solved at the moment can be exported in the hope that better options will be available when it reemerges. On some occasions, this move is calculated and strategic. More often, it is the result of lacking competences. Not knowing how to tackle a problem is a common reason for choosing to ignore it in favor of attending to problems within your areas of competence (Hertzum, 2008).

Third, uncoordinated system configurations or procedure adaptations can lead to exported problems. Such configurations and adaptations may solve immediate, local issues but cause problems in the long run because they disregard organization-wide issues (Torkilsheyggi and Hertzum, 2017). This reason for exported problem is particularly likely when local user groups are powerful and the implementation team is less so.

Fourth, problems are more likely to be exported, especially from the go-live phase, when the users lack technical interest, lack knowledge about how the system can be configured, lack the authority to propose procedure revisions, or lack incentives beyond getting today's work done. In these cases, the users will likely opt to accept functional, but suboptimal, ways of using the new system rather than to pursue the planned effects of the system.

As a concrete example of how exported problems can disturb and prolong go-live, Hertzum and Ellingsen (2019) investigate the implementation of Epic's electronic health record at a hospital in Denmark. The contract for the implementation of Epic at this and eleven other Danish hospitals amounted to DKK 2.8 billion (EUR 375 million). The vision for the new electronic health record was to eliminate paper records and replace a large number of existing clinical information systems with one integrated system. Epic went live at the hospital on May 21, 2016, following a big-bang strategy. However, the clinicians experienced multiple problems, their workload multiplied, the number of adverse events increased, the integration between Epic and some of the medical equipment malfunctioned, Epic occasionally duplicated medical orders, and many blood-test orders remained unsent because they were incomplete according to rules built into Epic. Often, the physicians did not understand why the blood-test orders were not sent, or they did not even realize that the orders had not been sent. In June 2018, two years after go-live, the system had not yet transitioned from stressful implementation to efficient routine use. Rather, an auditing report voiced sharp criticism and pinpointed that the experienced trouble was the result of exported problem:

- User training had started late, yet the system was still being modified during training. As a result, many users received training in a system dissimilar from the system they met at go-live.

- System testing had not been completed before go-live. As a result, the hospital had incomplete knowledge about whether the system fulfilled requirements or contained defects.

- The business case estimated a three-week productivity dip. This estimate was way too optimistic. As a result, the hospital was unprepared for the extent of the actual productivity dip.

- Benefits follow-up was put on hold in May 2017. As a result, it remained unknown to what extent planned benefits were being realized.

Appeals from a sizable group of chief physicians to abandon Epic received considerable press and some political support, but the system remained in mandatory use.

6.6   SUPER USERS

Super users are staff tasked with easing the users into their new ways of working. This task requires that the super users are knowledgeable about the new system and the procedures associated with it. Being users, they are also knowledgeable about the organization and primary work. During go-live, they are the users' first point of contact when the users experience problems. To fulfill this role most effectively, Obwegeser et al. (2019) recommend that super users should be at the same hierarchical level in the organization as the users. In addition, there must be a sufficient number of super users to respond quickly when users need support, especially during the first and most hectic period (Francoise et al., 2009). For this reason, external consultants from the preparation phase sometimes supplement the super users to provide extra support during this period. However, other organizations choose against consultants for go-live. As a symbolic indication that the organization is ready to run its new system on its own, they discontinue their consultants just before go-live (Brown and Vessey, 2001).

Through the on-site support they provide, super users are probably the most important booster of adoption during go-live. In addition, they are an important precaution against errors. Super users are hubs of advice, information, and reminders during a period where the users' old routines are no longer valid and new routines have yet to be established. The importance of super users warrants that management or the implementation team devotes considerable attention to their selection and training (Obwegeser et al., 2019). Super users do a better job if they are proactive ("I'll go see the users, in case they need me") than reactive ("If the users need me, they'll come see me"). Yuan et al. (2015) find that super users who volunteer for the role are more likely to be pro-active. Irrespective of whether super users are selected or volunteer for the role, the required skills resemble those for user representatives (Table 5.1).

Once identified, the super users must be trained in the system as well as the new procedures. For large systems, the training may involve a certification of the super users to ensure that they master the system at the level necessary to train and support their colleagues. Like the users, the super users need training in the system version that will become operational at go-live. Thus, the system must be finalized in time for the training of the super users, who must complete their own training before they can train the users. The resulting schedule is normally tight. User training is the super users' first task, followed by on-site support during go-live and further support during continued use; see Figure 6.4.

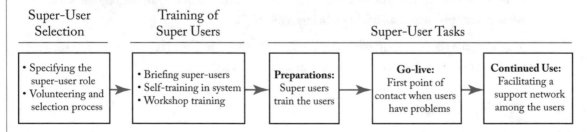

Figure 6.4: The selection, training, and tasks of super users.

By instructing the users or adjusting system settings, the super users will be able to handle many of the problems that cause the users uncertainty or prevent them from completing their tasks. The remaining problems must be escalated to the implementation team, system vendor, or organization management. This way, the super users serve as a link between the users and those responsible for the system and its implementation. The link is two-way in that those responsible receive information about the situation "on the ground" and the users receive solutions to their problems. To ensure effective communication, the super users often meet with the implementation team on a daily or weekly basis to gauge how the implementation is proceeding, discuss issues that slow it down, and coordinate troubleshooting activities (Culp et al., 2005). These meetings are also an opportunity for the super users to exchange information and solutions with each other.

Pan and Mao (2016) find that the super users' focus gradually widens. In the process, they stop merely identifying themselves with their business unit and become increasingly appreciative of the needs and practices of other units. That is, they become less representative of their business unit and more concerned with how the system serves the organization. If this shift in focus continues too far, then the users in the units may feel that their voice is no longer being heard. Accordingly, the implementation team may get inaccurate feedback and management may mistakenly come to believe that the system causes fewer problems and frustrations than the users actually experience. Pan and Mao (2016) also describe that it takes some time for the super users to transition from learning about the system to being sufficiently confident to start insisting on the need for system adaptations. This transition is especially difficult when management's rationale for the implementation is standardization. However, insisting on needed adaptations is essential to arriving at a system that fits the local particulars. If these adaptations were neglected in the preparation phase, they must be raised and resolved during go-live or continued use.

Go-live is a busy period for the super users, for two reasons. First, plenty of communication is needed to handle how-to questions, escalate problems that cannot be handled on the spot, inform users about workarounds to bypass temporary system defects, and so forth. With efficient communication, the users will experience frustration but they will also experience that support is in place to alleviate the frustrations. Second, super users are particularly well-suited for this communication role. Åsand and Mørch (2006) find that users prefer to interact with super users when they experience problems, rather than with technical IT staff. Thus, supplementing super users with other support staff is perceived negatively by the users. The super users' distinctive quality is that they are users themselves and, therefore, understand the primary work. The more hours super users spend in their super-user role, the more positively their colleagues perceive the new system (Halbesleben et al., 2009).

In some cases, the support provided by the super users is so good that new work roles emerge to make this support permanent. As a negative example, Reijonen and Heikkilä (2006) describe the partial adoption of a difficult-to-use system that was implemented with insufficient user training. To get their work done, the users noted task data on a piece of paper rather than entered the data directly into the system. Instead, the data were entered into the system later. During go-live, this workaround was necessary because the users needed a super user to support them in entering the data into the system. Later, the users had become accustomed to this practice and delegated the data entry to a clerk. However, the users' notes were often incomplete so that the clerk could not complete the data entry but had to get back to the users for additional information, thereby creating a cumbersome process and further delaying the entry of the data.

CHAPTER 7

Continuing Design During Use: The Long, Improvisational Process

After the hectic go-live period, the system enters continued use. This phase continues for as long as the system remains in operational use—years or even decades. While go-live was mainly about abrupt change, continued use is about numerous, mostly small, and evolutionary changes spread over a long period of time (By, 2005; Reich and Benbasat, 2000). Together, these changes may involve more work than the two preceding phases (Moon et al., 2018). Some of the changes will emerge within the organization, others will be triggered by organization-external events. For example, staggering technological developments happen in the timespan of a decade and call for organizations to respond. This way, the sheer length of continued use makes it important to organizational implementation, but the length of this phase also calls for another approach than the high-intensity implementation activities during go-live. Unless organizations find and establish such an approach, they will forgo opportunities to reap the full benefit of their systems.

This chapter starts by arguing the need for continuing the implementation activities during use (Section 7.1). The mutual adaptation of the system and organization continues beyond go-live because it involves the gradual realization of which affordances the system has—and lacks—in relation to the work performed in the organization. It is also when the system enters continued use that follow-up activities should be undertaken to ascertain whether the specified effects have been realized (Section 7.2). In addition, the organization should seek to learn why some effects remain unrealized and what other effects the system unexpectedly helps realize. Such learning involves heeding how users concretely work with and around the system to get their work done (Section 7.3). To discontinue inappropriate workarounds and derive benefit from the unanticipated opportunities afforded by the system, the organization must provide continual support for implementation activities (Section 7.4). This support depends on input from imaginative users, who tinker with the system and procedures. These tinkerers are key to the improvisational process of continuing design during use (Section 7.5).

7.1 DESIGN BEFORE USE OR DESIGN IN USE?

Wagner and Newell (2007) contend that continued use is the phase during which you can most effectively engage users in implementation activities. Their rationale for this contention is anchored in the practice view on organizational implementation (Figure 1.3). First, the users are primarily interested in getting their daily work done. The implementation of a new information system is a secondary concern for them. Second, the effect of the system on their daily work does not become salient to them until after go-live. During the preparations, the system is dissociated from the users' daily work; during go-live, their resources go into managing the transition. It is not until the system starts to enter continued use that the users get a stable sense of its consequences for their daily work. Many users are more motivated to influence the system and its use at this point than during the preparations. The result of this late motivation can be misalignment with implementation activities, which often assume that users provide their input during the preparations:

- To ensure the quality and legitimacy of the system, user participation in the preparations is important—but it may be difficult to obtain. The users are busy with their daily work and may be reluctant to devote sufficient time and attention to the implementation activities.

- To accommodate user requests after go-live, continual support is important—but it may be scarce. The implementation team has been scaled down and management may find that requests for adapting the system and organization should preferably have been made during the preparations.

Because organizational implementation is costly, "management usually is anxious to declare victory and move on to other things" (Ross, 1999, p. 67). In addition, organizations with a preference for planning may undervalue the improvisational process of continuing design during use. These organizations tend to approach change as episodic (Section 2.2). In contrast, organizations that view change as continuous more readily embrace an improvisational design-in-use process. No implementation team can plan everything ahead and anticipate all the ways in which a new system can and will affect the organization. Thus, all organizations would benefit from extending their support for implementation activities into continued use to seize the unanticipated opportunities that emerge over time (Boudreau and Robey, 2005; Wagner and Newell, 2007).

Different forms of prototyping have become common in technical development. Designers iteratively make still more refined prototypes and use them for generating feedback, improving designs, and setting directions. Wagner and Newell (2007) ask why organizational implementation should be any different. Off-the-shelf systems appear especially suited to a prototyping approach to organizational implementation because an operational system is available from the very beginning. This system could initially be implemented with basic functionality only and then iteratively extended by adding the modules that require more extensive configuration and work-practice changes. The extensions should be made when they provide functionality that users request. It may be possible to anticipate some of these requests; the others will be unanticipated. Over time, the unanticipated requests will likely outnumber the anticipated requests. The gradual implementation of requested functionality maintains a focus on the organization and the users' experienced needs.

Consistent with this approach, Heikkilä et al. (2003) propose that implementation should start with changing the organization, including the staff's thoughts about what is needed, and end with introducing new system functionality to support these changes.

It is striking how often the order is reversed, that is, how often a new system is introduced before the users have experienced, or expressed, a need for its functionality. A lot of the pressure on organizational implementations is brought about by the absence of an experienced need among the users. Shifting part of the focus from design-before-use planning to design-in-use improvisation eases the pressure on the preparations. You will no longer be expected to get everything right in the first attempt. More focus on design-in-use improvisation also recognizes that subsequent changes in technological possibilities, supplier infrastructures, customer expectations, market trends, or other environmental factors will call for organizational responses that involve reconfiguring the system and its use. The need for these reconfigurations will emerge over time, and many of them will initially be experienced by users as they go about using the system in their daily work. Over the years in which a system is in operational use, its users will see opportunities for using it in many new ways and for many additional purposes (Hertzum et al., 1993; Karasti et al., 2010; Ribes and Finholt, 2009). To seize these opportunities, the implementation activities must continue during use.

While the preparations lend themselves to a planned top-down approach, the improvisational continuation of implementation during use is a bottom-up process that acknowledges and depends on user input. Both preparation and improvisation are needed, but their combination can create tension. Some managers and users perceive design-in-use improvisation as an uncertain and unwelcome process that most of all points back to insufficient preparations (Hertzum and Torkilsheyggi, 2019; Wagner and Newell, 2007). These people tend to prefer a top-down approach in which others plan in detail how the new system should be used. However, they may at the same time be quick to criticize the system and implementation process when they after go-live experience that some of their needs are not met. Organizations that plan to rely on thorough preparations should realize that unanticipated consequences and reactions will happen anyway. They should specifically be aware that the absence of critical voices during the preparations is no guarantee that the users will be satisfied once the system is put into operational use. Critical voices and requests for adaptations may emerge at that point.

Other managers and users welcome the continuation of the implementation activities during use, for at least three reasons. First, the continuation of the implementation activities after go-live implies a more gradual change process in which the users and their ways of working coevolve with the system (Wagner and Newell, 2007). This way, the users get more time to absorb the changes and learn the new ways of working. Second, the users discover—through experimentation and exploration—how the system enables them to work more effectively and are motivated by these discoveries (Germonprez et al., 2011). This way, the new ways of working are adopted out of appreciation for how they facilitate the users' work, rather than as procedures that must be remembered and complied with. Third, the users perceive the continued implementation activities as an acknowledgment that those who concretely use the system have something to offer (Hertzum and Torkilsheyggi, 2019). Some of the users embrace this opportunity to contribute by tinkering with the system.

A planned top-down process and an improvisational bottom-up process should not be seen as alternatives. Rather, they complement each other so that organizational control has an inverted U-shaped influence on adoption (Maas et al., 2014). That is, the optimum is a medium level of control that combines top-down planning with bottom-up improvisation. A key issue in finding this optimal level of control is to establish a shared long-term vision that maintains focus in the improvisational process without stifling it.

7.2   FOLLOWING UP ON EFFECTS REALIZATION

The productivity dip after go-live shows that a system does not immediately and inevitably yield benefit for the organization (Section 6.4). To achieve the effects that motivate the introduction of the system, you need to follow up on their realization. Therefore, effects specification includes specifying the follow-up activities to be performed by the implementation team to ascertain whether the effect has been realized (Figure 5.2). It is not sufficient to specify what you want to achieve with the new system and then assume that it will happen by itself when the system goes live. Without follow-up, there is considerable risk that the benefits will be delayed or remain unrealized (Einhorn et al., 2019; Hertzum and Simonsen, 2011; Irani, 2010).

In spite of this risk, effects follow-up is often omitted. For example, Einhorn et al. (2019) find that only one third of organizations follows up on whether the benefits specified in information-systems business cases are realized. A further third makes a business case to win approval for the system by specifying the expected benefits, but do not follow up on their realization after the system has been implemented. The last third of organizations implements their systems without first making a business case. This way, benefits may not be realized because the organization remains unaware of their status and of the barriers that must be surmounted to realize the benefits. Not using the business case for follow-up also increases the risk of overoptimistic business cases because there is little risk of being caught promising too much. Adoption decisions made on the basis of such business cases can result in disappointment when promised benefits do not materialize.

To assess the effects of a new system, you need to know how the organization performs before and after implementation. This knowledge can be obtained by measuring performance after implementation and comparing it with measurements made before implementation, or it can be obtained by retrospectively asking knowledgeable staff how post-implementation performance compares to pre-implementation performance. The former requires quantifiable effects, the latter may be subject to forgetting and wishful thinking. In both cases, follow-up is neither easy nor perfect, but it is vastly preferable to no follow-up. For anything but small-scale systems, before and after measurements are recommended (Hertzum and Simonsen, 2011; Irani, 2010; Wei, 2008).

The before measurements must be conducted in the preparation phase while the old system is still in use and the users' perception of it has not yet been biased by their expectations regarding the new system. The after measurements are conducted after go-live. In between before and after measurements, pilot implementations provide an opportunity for obtaining early indications of the after measurements by measuring the effect of the system at the pilot site. The implementation team should repeat the after measurements until the specified effects have been realized, or abandoned (Einhorn et al., 2019; Francoise et al., 2009; Simonsen and Hertzum, 2012).

Hertzum and Simonsen (2011) recommend making effects a central instrument in guiding the technical development and organizational implementation of information systems. The recommended process consists of effects specification, effects realization, and effects follow-up; see Figure 7.1. Effects follow-up may reveal that a pursued effect has not been attained. If the effect is still considered desirable, then the implementation team continues with renewed activities to realize the effect. However, the effects follow-up may also reveal a negative side effect of the specified effects or lead to the identification of a hitherto unspecified, yet desirable, effect of using the system. If so, you should revise the effects specification because the reason why the system is adopted has changed. While the loop back to effects realization focuses on the planned change, the loop back to effects specification allows for the incorporation of new opportunities that emerge with changing business conditions. The process bears some resemblance to that of single-loop and double-loop learning (Figure 2.2).

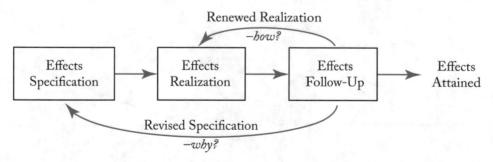

Figure 7.1: Effects-driven development and implementation, based on Hertzum and Simonsen (2011).

The data needed for follow-up will often be available in the old and new system. When this is the case, the implementation team simply needs to extract and compare these data. In other cases, the follow-up data consist of input from the users, such as their ratings of data completeness, error rates, and response times to customers (Wei, 2008). Depending on the specified effects, you may also ask users to rate their personal experience of using the system, such as their mental workload or job satisfaction. You need to collect these data from the users before and after the implementation of the new system. In the remaining cases, measurements must be made to obtain the follow-up data. These measurements can take a variety of forms. In the following, two of the effect examples from Section 5.3 are used to illustrate how the implementation team can obtain follow-up data through measurements.

The first example concerns the effect that all information about medication is recorded in the electronic medication record (Granlien and Hertzum, 2009). The follow-up consisted of medical record audits, which involve that the content of the records is retrospectively assessed. Medical record audits have the advantage that they can be conducted without disturbing the clinicians' daily work. Each audit spanned records from seven consecutive days and established the number of violations of the requirement to record all medication information in the electronic medication record. The first two audits were conducted before go-live to establish a baseline. The third audit was conducted shortly after go-live and showed the need for renewed realization activities. Two extra realization activities were conducted: one educational activity (a how-to pocket guide with annotated screenshots from the system) and one purely motivational activity (a box of candy with a message on the lid reminding the clinicians about the effect). The fourth and fifth audit showed that these extra activities were successful and the effect attained. However, the sixth audit, conducted to assess long-term effects realization, raised some concern that the effect might be wearing off after the end of the activities to realize it; see Figure 7.2. Without the sixth audit, the hospital would not have known that additional realization activities were probably needed.

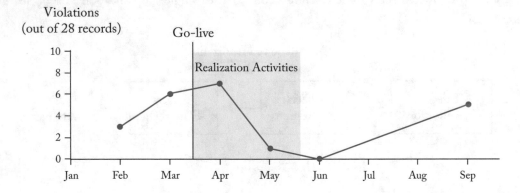

Figure 7.2: Follow-up for the effect that all information about medication is recorded in the electronic medication record (EMR), based on Granlien and Hertzum (2009). Each of the 6 audits involved the medical records of 28 patients and established how many of these records that violated the requirement for all medication information to be recorded in the EMR.

The second example illustrates the comprehensive measurements undertaken to follow up on the effect that physicians and nurses in the emergency department spend more of their time with the patients (Hertzum and Simonsen, 2013). To achieve this effect, a wall-mounted electronic display with selected patient information was implemented to improve the clinicians' overview of their work. The follow-up consisted of tracking the whereabouts of the physicians and nurses for a four-week period before go-live and for another four-week period four months after go-live. The physicians and nurses who consented to take part in the follow-up wore a tag that emitted an ultrasound signal every 20 seconds. On the basis of these signals, it was determined whether they were in a patient room, in the clinicians' area, or in another part of the hospital; see Table 7.1. After the implementation of the overview displays, the physicians did not spend more of their time in the patient rooms with the patients. In retrospect, this non-change was considered understandable because most emergency-department physicians are junior and frequently need to consult with their colleagues. Thus, this effect was abandoned. In contrast, the nurses spent substantially more time with the patients after the implementation of the overview display. The 11 percentage-point increase corresponded to about 44 minutes per nurse shift. The emergency department was pleased with the realization of this effect.

Table 7.1: Follow-up for the effect that physicians and nurses spend more of their time with the patients, based on Hertzum and Simonsen (2013). Each column shows the percentage of time spent in patient rooms, in the clinicians' area, and in other locations

Location	Physicians (N = 316 shifts)		Nurses (N = 347 shifts)	
	Before	After	Before	After
Patient rooms	19%	20%	17%	28%
Clinicians' area	52%	59%	55%	44%
Other location	29%	20%	27%	28%

Immediately after go-live, the organization rarely needs follow-up data. The organization is experiencing a productivity dip and it is evident that the specified effects have not yet been realized. Follow-up becomes relevant a couple of months after go-live (Ward and Daniel, 2012). If follow-up data are easy to collect, then it is recommendable to start following up during the productivity dip to obtain data about how quickly the organization recovers from the productivity dip. If it is resource demanding to collect the follow-up data, then the follow-up can be postponed until it is estimated that the organization has recovered from go-live. Often, more resources will be required to collect the data for following up on some effects than others. In these cases, you should start follow-up earlier for the effects that are easier to collect data about. Subsequently, these data can enter into deciding when to follow up on the remaining effects.

To avoid swamping the organization with activities to collect follow-up data, the number of effects should be kept modest (Wei, 2008). Many effects are interlinked or overlapping due to the effects hierarchy (Figure 5.1). By focusing the follow-up activities on the middle-level effects, the implementation team can often infer that certain upper-level and lower-level effects are also attained. This reduces the amount of follow-up data that need to be collected. In addition, it is important to establish a constructive atmosphere around the follow-up activities. They are performed to obtain benefit from the system, not to blame the users for imperfect compliance with procedures. When the users work around the system, it is normally an indication that it fits their work poorly. Thus, it is an opportunity for learning about useful reconfigurations and, possibly, for revising the effects.

7.3   WORKAROUNDS

Workarounds are goal-driven changes to the procedures associated with the use of a system. They are performed by users to bypass or minimize the impact of obstacles that are perceived by the users as preventing them from getting their work done in a way that meets organizational and personal goals (Alter, 2014). On the one hand, workarounds are instances of non-compliance with the procedures for how to use the new system. From this perspective, workarounds call for renewed activities to increase adoption by changing the users' perception of the obstacles, insisting that the users abandon the workarounds, or incentivizing full adoption. Otherwise, the organization will not reap the full benefit of its new system. On the other hand, workarounds are indications of a poor fit between the system and the conditions under which the users perform their work. From this perspective, workarounds reveal additional needs and opportunities for adapting the system and procedures to the organization. Unless these adaptations are made, the organization will not reap the full benefit of the system. These two perspectives on workarounds are clearly at odds.

It is, however, not always obvious whether a workaround is dysfunctional or beneficial to the organization. For example, a workaround may be beneficial in the important sense of getting today's work done and, at the same time, dysfunctional in the important sense of increasing the long-term risk of errors. In deciding whether a workaround is dysfunctional or beneficial, the implementation team should consider that workarounds occur for multiple reasons, including the following (Alter, 2014; Beerepoot et al., 2019; Ferneley and Sobreperez, 2006):

- when users face situations, such as exceptions and anomalies, that are not covered by the system or procedures;

- when the new system renders an activity unnecessary but procedures still require that the activity is performed;

- when the people who should perform a task are unavailable and the task is instead performed by users who are not formally entitled to perform it;

- when the system requires input in a sequence or at a time that clashes with other task demands;

- when users perceive system workflows or mandated procedures as too cumbersome and slow;

- when the system malfunctions, lacks functionality, or generates more feedback messages than the users can process;

- when information that the users deem important cannot be entered into the system because it lacks appropriate input fields or the users lack access rights;

- when personal goals, such as individual performance or job satisfaction, conflict with organizational goals, such as revenue or standardization; and

- when users feel motivated to bypass or undermine decisions and requirements imposed by, for example, management.

The reasons at the top of the list concern workarounds that are essential for getting the daily work done. These workarounds may, however, go unnoticed in implementation activities because the users perceive them as unremarkable features of establishing new work routines. The reasons at the end of the list concern workarounds that are clearly undesirable for the organization because they seek to counterimplement the system. These workarounds will likely be exercised covertly and may, therefore, also go unnoticed in implementation activities. Because workarounds have considerable influence on system success, it is important that the implementation team seeks to become aware of, learn from, and act on them.

Workarounds complement the planned change by coping with the unanticipated consequences of the system, thereby embracing emergent change. The unanticipated consequences may emerge long after go-live and they can be positive as well as negative. While negative consequences lead to workarounds that seek to enable the organization to operate despite obstacles, the positive consequences lead to workarounds that seek to exploit these unanticipated opportunities. For example, Aanestad et al. (2017) describe how the use of a teleconferencing system implemented to facilitate collaboration among distributed healthcare staff was extended to include communication with isolation patients. Initially, a patient who had been in isolation for a long time wished to participate in patient-teaching sessions and to meet other patients at the hospital. While the patient's isolation status had hitherto made such activities impossible, the hospital provided the patient with an iPad that had a videoconference connection to the teaching room. Later, isolation patients also used the iPad to communicate with the healthcare staff outside of the isolation room. This extension in the use of the teleconferencing system happened several years after it was initially implemented and was made possible by technological enhancements of the system in the intervening period.

A frequent negative consequence of workarounds is that they focus on resolving local issues to the extent of creating problems in other parts of the organization. As an example, Maas et al. (2016) describe how a planned system update introduced a requirement for package labels to include a barcode as well as an article code. The business unit responsible for packaging had to add the article code but there was not much room for it on the labels. They worked around this problem by shrinking the barcode and adding the article code next to it. This way, the packages were labeled correctly. However, the units receiving the packages were unable to scan the barcodes because they were too small and too close to the article codes. Consequently, they had to type the barcodes into the system by hand, thereby delaying the processing of all incoming packages. While this workaround should obviously be revoked, it is often difficult to revoke workarounds once they have become part of routine practice. Even if a workaround is revoked, you need to be effective in your communication to convey that the additional workarounds it necessitated (e.g., typing the barcode into the system by hand) can also be revoked.

In their essence, workarounds are instances of situated learning about how to incorporate the new system in local practices. That is, they are resources for fine-tuning the organizational implementation in a design-in-use manner. Safadi and Faraj (2010) propose that workarounds evolve in four stages. First, workarounds arise when users perceive, correctly or incorrectly, that their needs are not met by the new system. Second, workarounds crystallize as the individual users gain more experience with the system and become more settled in their ways of using it. Third, workarounds diffuse informally among users and, possibly, gain traction and become shared local practices. Fourth, workarounds inform implementation activities by providing feedback and opportunities for formal adjustments to the system and procedures. While workarounds predominantly arise and crystallize as a result of individual users' tinkering with the system, their diffusion and formalization are social processes that depend on effective communication networks. The implementation team should tap and facilitate these social processes. In addition, the organization should provide long-term support for tinkering.

7.4   CONTINUAL SUPPORT FOR IMPLEMENTATION ACTIVITIES

The organizational implementation of an information system is often thought of as a project, thereby suggesting that it is a temporary activity with an end date (Markus, 2004). This project approach has its roots in the system view on organizational implementation. From a practice view, organizational implementation is an open-ended process of design in use. During this process, the use of the system will evolve to derive planned benefits from it, but the system will also be bundled with other goals in the organization and included in the activities to realize them. It is through this bundling that the system becomes integrated in the organization (Elbanna, 2010). The bundling happens when users see and pursue additional opportunities with the system. However, these visionary users need organizational support. Otherwise, the system will struggle because too many reasons to adopt it remain unrealizable or are only utilized by few users.

The basic challenge in providing organizational support for continuing design in use is to remain committed to the pursuit of opportunities for deriving additional benefit from the system. At an abstract level, this commitment means that the organization exercises collective mindfulness (Aanestad and Jensen, 2016): The organization is sensitive to how it operates, reluctant to resort to simplified modes of understanding, preoccupied with detecting indicators of trouble, and open to change its ways of working to sustain operations. Concretely, the organizational implementation must transition from a project responsible for the preparations and go-live to a platform for facilitating design-in-use activities.

The platform consists of a standing team that facilitates the design-in-use activities initiated by users. These activities will often cut across systems in ways that are determined by task needs rather than aligned with system boundaries. The promise of design in use lies as much in the connections among different systems as in the possibilities within the new system (Arvidsson and Mønsted, 2018). Therefore, the platform should not be restricted to the new system only, but facilitate its integration into the array of systems involved in the users' work. To nurture and benefit from such integrations, the platform should be an innovation forum for turning practices that emerge locally into system uses that are shared across business units. There are six elements to this platform.

First, it involves *scouting for workarounds and goals with which the new system can be bundled*. Scouting serves for the organization—as opposed to individual users—to become aware of additional opportunities with the system and of undesirable uses of it (Elbanna, 2010). In the period immediately after go-live, the super users can do such scouting as part of their on-site support. When on-site support ends, scouting should however continue because workarounds and opportunities for bundling will emerge over time, for example in response to organization external events. In selecting people for scouting, it is important to select people who embrace the proactive nature of scouting. It involves curiosity and an outgoing approach to learn about how the system is used. According to project managers, the unplanned uses of implemented systems are about evenly divided between desirable uses that should be promoted and undesirable uses that should be discontinued (White and Fortune, 2002); other studies find few undesirable uses (e.g., Germonprez et al., 2011). If the scouts are super users, they will often lack the organizational power necessary to enforce the discontinuation of undesirable uses. Instead, the scouts must escalate cases of undesirable use to managers. Escalation must be handled sensitively to avoid that it eliminates the users' preparedness to tell the scout how they actually use the system.

Second, *new uses of the system must be allowed to grow*. Initially, most new uses will be immature ideas that inspire their innovator but lack the clarity necessary to convince others of their potential. If the scouts approach an innovative user too early, then the new idea will easily end up disregarded. It may, for example, be disregarded because it involves a deviation from procedures or a change in the business goals pursued by the organization. To cultivate new ideas at this early stage, the staff must have the freedom to pursue new ideas. Often, users will obtain this freedom by concealing their activities and, thereby, flying under the radar (Arvidsson and Mønsted, 2018). The platform for facilitating design-in-use activities should allow for such concealing. At the next stage, selected users may formally be granted the freedom to pursue an idea by creating an incubator project that temporarily shields the development of the idea from the sanctions to which it would otherwise be exposed (Burke and Morley, 2016). In addition to developing the idea, the incubator project is an opportunity to showcase the idea and generate momentum by winning support for it from management and prospective users.

Third, the continual implementation support must involve *support for system reconfigurations*. Users will often have the organizational and work-domain knowledge necessary to see additional opportunities with the system but lack the technical knowledge or access rights to adapt the system to these opportunities. To benefit from these opportunities, the organization must make resources for changing the system available on the shop floor (Dittrich et al., 2017). Provided the system is configurable, such shop-floor resources may consist of super users who have received training in configuring the system. The advantage of super users is that they are users and internal to the organization. That is, they are easy to approach because they understand the organization and primary work (Maas et al., 2016). To enable changes beyond the super users' capabilities, it should be considered to provide the users with some level of access to the system vendor's technical developers. This access should be filtered through management for approval, but it should provide for making smallish changes quickly. Otherwise, the users lose interest or invent less efficient workarounds. Larger changes require a more formal approach and should be handled as self-contained projects. Because the innovation potential in the new uses of the system lies as much in connecting it with other systems, these projects and configuration activities will often involve changes in multiple systems.

Fourth, in parallel with the support for system reconfigurations, the organization should provide continual *support for organizational adaptations*. While users may foster ideas about beneficial organizational adaptations, they will often lack the authority to institute changes in procedures, especially if the scope of these changes reaches beyond their unit (Torkilsheyggi and Hertzum, 2017). Thus, support for organizational adaptations requires that the organization is able and willing to put managerial weight behind ideas that emerge bottom up. Agile organizations do this well; bureaucratic organizations find it more difficult. Aanestad et al. (2017) describe how an organization set up a permanent team with the responsibility of continually developing the use of a system that was deemed of strategic importance. This team was supported by a network of coordinators, who scouted for new ideas and disseminated information about new system facilities.

Fifth, the implementation support should involve *quality assessment of the technical and organizational adaptations made by users*. Users tend to be overconfident in the quality of their system reconfigurations, which often contain errors (Ko et al., 2011; Powell et al., 2008). Similarly, the users' organizational adaptations may contain errors. Typical reasons for errors are insufficient technical competences or an overly local perspective on organizational processes. To capture and correct the errors, the quality of user-made adaptations should be audited, at least if the adaptations concern critical processes or will be disseminated to many users. The adaptations can also lead to the specification of new effects and be included in the follow-up activities on effects realization (Section 7.2). In bureaucratic organizations, there is a risk that the auditing becomes time-consuming for the users. If this risk can be avoided, the users will appreciate the division of labor because it allows them to create adaptations informally and then hand them over to a team that handles quality assurance (Vogelsmeier et al., 2008).

Sixth, users may form informal user forums for exchanging information and tips about the system (Maas et al., 2016). *These user forums should be organizationally acknowledged* for their long-term contribution to the dissemination of help with using the system. Because the user forums emerge to discuss issues that are salient to the users, the users may be more motivated to participate than during user training (Boudreau and Robey, 2005). As a result, user forums have, for example, been found to produce manuals with handy information for doing common tasks or remembering rarely used settings. Apart from providing information and tips, user forums also exert social influence by making system use the norm. This norm likely allows for workarounds but they will be socially vetted and, thus, unlikely to prioritize individual users' goals over organizational goals. The organization has a strong interest in well-functioning user forums and should support these forums by granting users the time to participate and by attending to issues raised by the forums.

To be effective, the platform for continual implementation support must be competently staffed. The implementation team may remain staffed for a couple of weeks or month after go-live as a precaution against errors, but then its members will be on to other projects or redeployed back to their business units. It quickly becomes the situation that few people know first-hand why the system is configured exactly the way it is. A former implementation-team member puts it succinctly (Norton et al., 2012, p. 655): "*You find that Fred learnt it and he left and he told Bert, well he told Bert a percentage of what he knew and Bert left and he told Alf and Alf only knows a percentage of what Bert knew, then he told Betty and so on.*" To counter this knowledge loss, the organization should make the continual implementation support an attractive work task that the platform team sees as a long-term appointment. Super users often have a key role in ensuring the continuity and quality of the continual implementation support (Maas et al., 2016; Norton et al., 2012; Obwegeser et al., 2019).

7.5   TINKERERS

The tinkerers are the users who engage in design in use. They are the key group of people in the long, improvisational implementation process that accompanies continued use. Without tinkerers, the implementation process would end with the troubleshooting activities after go-live and there would be no input to the continual implementation support. It is the tinkerers who—over time—see the emergent opportunities afforded by the system and pursue them by using the system in unplanned ways (Orlikowski, 1996), bundling it with other goals (Elbanna, 2010), working around its limitations (Alter, 2014), and in other ways forging new processes through experimentation and exploration (Avgerou et al., 2009).

Most users do not tinker. The continued implementation activities are dependent on the minority who do. While most users merely seek to exploit a new system by using it for specified purposes, tinkerers also explore the new system to derive additional benefit from it. Their explorations generate variation in the use of the system and, thereby, create possibilities for spotting the better ways of exploiting the system (Lavie et al., 2010). The time at which people adopt new ideas captures their overall attitude toward new technologies. It characterizes tinkerers that they are quick to adopt and adapt new ideas. Rogers (2003) distinguishes among five adopter categories; see Figure 7.3. They are as follows.

- *Innovators* are venturesome, like to try out new things, and are the first to adopt new technologies. They mostly interact with other innovators and, therefore, have limited direct influence on how the community of users in an organization perceives and uses a new system.

- The *early adopters* are a larger group than the innovators and more integrated in the local social context than the innovators. The early adopters are respected by their peers as the go-to persons for questions about new technology. Thereby, they exert a high degree of opinion leadership.

- The *early majority* adopts technologies before the average user and constitutes a numerous category. They are rarely opinion leaders but interact frequently with their peers. Thus, they tend to be well-informed about workarounds and other changes to systems and procedures.

- The *late majority* is also a numerous category. They approach technologies with some skepticism and defer adoption longer than the average user. Due to their skepticism, their adoption is often the result of increasing peer pressure. They do not explore a system for new or smarter uses.

- *Laggards* prefer the tried-and-tested solutions and tend to be suspicious of new technologies. They mostly interact with others who also hold traditional values, and they are easily put off by arguments about innovation and change. Laggards are the last to adopt a technology.

Tinkerers are mostly innovators and early adopters. That is, it is only about one in six users who tinker (Figure 7.3). Innovators are often assumed to be "ahead of the trend" (von Hippel, 1986) in the sense that their use of a system is seen as indicative of how the broader user community will come to use the system at some later point. On the one hand, this assumption suggests that implementing the innovators' ideas about how to use the system will accelerate the transition to smarter ways of working. On the other hand, there is a risk that the broader user community is not yet ready for the innovators' ideas and rejects them. This risk is smaller if the continued implementation activities are based on the early adopters' ideas. The reason for the reduced risk is, partly, that the early adopters are more similar to the early and late majority and, partly, that their frequent opinion leadership adds weight to their ideas.

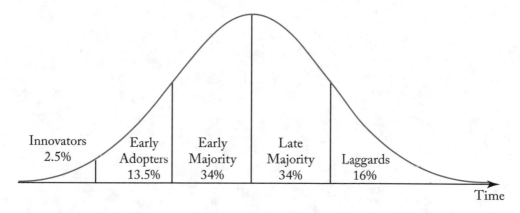

Figure 7.3: The five adopter categories, based on Rogers (2003). By definition, the innovators are the first 2.5% to adopt a technology. Similarly, the remaining adopter categories are defined as a specified percentage of the total user population.

To make the most of the tinkerers, you must nurture them. This nurturing involves creating a culture that promotes tinkering by empowering the users. One element in such empowerment is to provide users with access to the configuration facilities in their systems. If users feel empowered by a system, they incorporate it more fully into their practices (Maas et al., 2014). However, many organizations restrict access to configuration facilities to obtain standardization, avoid errors, and preclude security breaches. Restricting the tinkerers' degrees of freedom is most relevant if the system is safety-critical or has complexly interdependent components. Another element in empowering the tinkerers is the platform for continual implementation support, see Section 7.4. This platform amplifies the reach and impact of their efforts by making resources and competences available (Dittrich et al., 2017). In addition, it provides possibilities for quality assurance and shows the tinkerers that their ideas are valued by the organization.

CHAPTER 8

The Larger Picture and the Local Needs

The three phases of preparations, go-live, and continuing design during use involve a range of activities within the organization that implements a new information system. However, organizations interact with their environment, and their information systems are part of these interactions. Thus, the implementation of an information system transcends the organization and reaches into its environment (Monteiro et al., 2013). Organizational implementation may, for example, include realigning procedures with strategic partners, reallocating tasks among subcontractors, complying with new legislation, adopting industry standards, and responding to market trends. These issues insert the local implementation activities in a larger picture, which underscores their complexity and the diverse competences needed to handle them successfully.

This concluding chapter starts by providing an outlook to two aspects of the larger picture. First, some systems reach more broadly and deeply into their environment than others. These systems have infrastructural properties, which add to the complexities of their organizational implementation (Section 8.1). Second, some system vendors involve their client community in generification activities (Section 8.2). These activities are important for the individual client because they determine how the base system evolves. That is, they determine which currently unmet needs the system will meet in future releases. The larger picture influences how users perceive the implementation of a new system (Section 8.3). Their perception of the implementation is also influenced by local issues such as the implementation process. To run the implementation process well, the implementation team must have the necessary competences. The chapter ends by cataloging these competences (Section 8.4).

8.1 SYSTEMS WITH INFRASTRUCTURAL PROPERTIES

Systems differ in scale, scope, and longevity. Scale is about the number of business units or departments spanned by a system. Some systems are intra-departmental, others are organization-wide, and still others are inter-organizational. Scope is about the diversity and interconnectedness of the goals, or processes, to which a system contributes. Some systems have large scale but modest scope—they serve the same goal across many business units. Other systems serve multiple, interconnected goals in a single business unit. Still other systems have extensive scale as well as extensive scope. Longevity is about the duration for which a system is in operational use. Some systems have more history than others or a longer projected future. With increasing scale, scope, and longevity, a system increasingly becomes an infrastructure (Star and Ruhleder, 1996). Systems with infrastructural properties are more complex to implement because they require that more people adopt, because they reach into more organizational processes, and because they affect practices with more history. Four consequences should be noted by implementation teams.

First, the extra complexity becomes noticeable as soon as a system extends beyond a single business unit. As a result, unanticipated complications often ensue when locally successful systems are scaled up to organization-wide use. Rasmussen et al. (2010) describe a system for presenting selected patient information on large, wall-mounted displays. The system was developed in collaboration with emergency departments (EDs) and successfully implemented in the EDs of four hospitals. With the system, the ED clinicians' overview of their work improved (Hertzum, 2011) and the ED nurses spent more time with the patients (Table 7.1). The ED clinicians also derived other benefits from the system by tinkering extensively with it. Based on the success of the system in the EDs, one of the hospitals decided to extend it to the entire hospital (Torkilsheyggi and Hertzum, 2017). Three years after the system was introduced in the ED, networked displays were mounted on the walls in all departments to support both intra- and interdepartmental coordination.

However, the system saw little use outside the ED. The department managers did not perceive an urgent need for the system and prioritized other activities. The super users configured the system for their departments but lacked the authority, knowledge, and inclination to implement interdepartmental adaptations of the system and procedures. The clinicians remained uncertain about the system and mostly reacted by waiting for their colleagues to adopt. Hospital management introduced standardization that involved partly rolling back the department-specific configurations made by the super users, who became demotivated (Torkilsheyggi and Hertzum, 2017). In sum, the implementation process, which had been energetic and innovative in the ED, congealed before the non-ED clinicians experienced the system as useful. After several attempts to revive the organization-wide implementation, it was abandoned.

Second, systems with infrastructural properties grow through extensions and evolutions; they are not implemented from scratch. The large-display system was already running in the ED; scaling it up merely consisted of configuring it for the other departments. Relatedly, most organizations already have a personnel management system; increasing its scope merely involves extending it, for example with a module for feeding information to letter templates or to the staff page on the company intranet. The longevity of these systems means that new modules and uses are implemented in a design-in-use manner—the systems grow. Each extension with a new module may be organized as an implementation project, but it is the series of projects that determines the direction in which the system evolves. This introduces a need for cross-project planning. Without such planning, individual projects may make decisions that are sensible in the context of the project but shortsighted from the perspective of evolving the system in the desired direction (Karasti et al.,

2010). Cross-project planning is challenging because it requires a long-term vision for the system. To maintain a long-term vision, organizations should periodically revisit effects specification and effects follow-up (Sections 5.3 and 7.2), particularly for systems with infrastructural properties.

Third, the implementation of most systems with extensive scale and scope involves adoption at multiple sites that each has its own management. As a result, there is no one management that can make implementation-wide decisions about the system and its use. The absence of one controlling management is most evident for inter-organizational systems. For example, Askedal et al. (2019, p. 73) find that the partners in the implementation of an inter-organizational system "acknowledged the importance of what they could achieve together" but at the same time "struggled to see immediate benefits for their individual organizations." In such a setting, implementation problems are likely because the collective benefit of the system is not owned by one controlling management. Instead, the collective benefit easily becomes secondary to the absence of individual benefits, thereby complicating the work of the implementation team. Many of the problems seen for inter-organizational systems recur for interdepartmental systems. While these systems in principle have a controlling top management, department management often has considerable autonomy in practice. Rohde and Wulf (2018) find that department structures often hinder an organization-wide mandate for change because the departments have conflicting interests and act on them. Similarly, Ali and Miller (2017) identify interdepartmental conflicts as a key barrier to implementation success.

Fourth, even industry-level changes can sometimes be accomplished. While systems with infrastructural properties introduce additional complexity, they also make it possible to tackle larger problems. To achieve profound change, you may need to engage dauntingly complex infrastructures. Apple's involvement in the distribution and consumption of music provides an illustrative example (Isaacson, 2011).

Mobile, digital music players had been around for some time when Apple launched the iPod in 2001. What made the iPod special was its simplicity, which to a large extent was achieved by making it a device merely for playing music. To organize music, that is to make play lists, the users had to use iTunes on their computer and then synchronize with their iPod. With the iPod and iTunes, users had an integrated environment for playing and organizing their music. But they did not have a similarly simple, and legal, way of getting new music. To the detriment of the music industry, many users resorted to downloading illegal copies of music from free file-sharing services. In an effort to combat illegal downloading, iTunes was integrated with an online music shop, iTunes Store. Through agreements with major record labels, their music was available in iTunes Store and they got paid when users bought it in the store.

The final system consisting of iPod, iTunes, and iTunes Store (Figure 8.1) served millions of users with multiple interconnected goals. Implementing this infrastructure involved changing the way people consumed music, the way record labels distributed music, and the way musicians got paid for their music. Individually, none of the three components of the system could have achieved these changes. The changes were achieved by bundling multiple goals, establishing inter-organizational collaborations, exploiting existing technologies, seeing market opportunities, and pursuing long-term visions.

iPod   iTunes   iTunes Store

Figure 8.1: An infrastructure that changed the music industry—Apple's iPod, iTunes, and iTunes Store.

8.2   GENERIFICATION: VENDORS INVOLVING CLIENTS IN SYSTEM EVOLUTION

Organizational implementation requires systems that can be adapted to the organization. To meet this requirement for localization, system vendors engage in generification (Pollock et al., 2007). Through generification, vendors extend their systems in directions that make the systems adaptable to the needs of more clients. Thereby, vendors aim to retain their current clients as well as to make their systems attractive to new clients. Vendors are often not making a profit from the first client for which they develop a new system, so they are dependent on subsequently selling it to more clients. These clients have some overlapping needs but also some discrepant needs—hence the requirement for localization. In contrast to localization, generification is not directed at any one client in particular. Rather, it is about synthesizing the needs of multiple clients into extensions that hence make the system more valuable to the community of clients.

Generification emphasizes that the relation between the client organization and its vendor exists in the context of the relations between the vendor and its other clients. That is, the system has infrastructural properties that reach beyond its implementation in the individual client organization and, instead, reflect how the system is shaped by the community of clients. Many vendors ask their clients for input to the generification activities. This way, your continued implementation activities are extended with an organization-external activity that involves building relations with other clients. There are several aspects to this activity (Haines, 2009; Johannessen and Ellingsen, 2009; Pollock et al., 2007).

- Participation in generification activities, such as client workshops, provides opportunities for learning from other clients. While the workshop is arranged by the vendor, these opportunities are otherwise independent of the vendor. The clients exchange information about current use practices, solutions to shared problems, and visions for deriving additional benefit from the system.

- Participation in generification activities is also an opportunity to influence the vendor. To exert influence, clients—especially smaller clients—need to form alliances. System extensions promoted by a group of clients carry more weight and are more likely to generalize to future clients. Conversely, a major client can try to promote its needs by forming a strategic partnership with the vendor.

- If a client succeeds in turning its needs into the system default, then that client is freed from the configuration activities otherwise needed to adapt the system to the client organization. Being freed from these activities expedites the implementation of new system releases and, thereby, simplifies the continued implementation process. Other clients may have to devote considerable resources to configuring each new release.

- By involving the clients in balancing their needs against one another, some of the responsibility for which system extensions to prioritize is shifted away from the vendor. This shift instills a longer-term perspective among the clients. As a result, the clients focus more on the overall direction in which the system gradually evolves and less on the concrete extensions included in its next release.

- Vendors—especially smaller vendors—are not just involving their clients in generification activities, they are also themselves clients in other vendors' generification activities. These second-order generification activities for example determine the possibilities for interfacing a system with other vendors' systems. The presence or absence of such interfaces influences how well the system can be adapted to the client organization.

The decision to implement a system initiates a relation with its vendor. This relation is affected by the vendor's market position and by the position the client organization can hope to attain in the client community. Considerations about this relation should be part of the management adoption process (Figure 3.1). Vendor selection is important because the long-term implementation process during continued use is dependent on how the vendor extends the system over time, not just on what the system looks like when initially acquired. The impact of the long-term implementation process increases with the scale, scope, and longevity of the system.

8.3   USER PERCEPTIONS OF ORGANIZATIONAL IMPLEMENTATION

The large number of challenged and failed implementations (Fitzgerald et al., 2014; Standish Group, 2020) shows that users often have negative experiences with new information systems, at least during the shakedown period. It also shows a gap between management's perception of the new system and the users' perception of it: Management's perception led to a decision to adopt the system, whereas the users' perception of it resulted in partial adoption or even non-use.

The users' perception of the implementation of a new system obviously depends on how the system changes their work, but it also depends on the implementation process. During the preparations, inadequate communication and user participation are common sources of frustration among the users. These sources of frustration remain important after go-live, but others are added. One of the new sources of user frustration is to wait a long time for support. Another is to experience the same system error again after having reported it. In addition, Spencer (2015) documents user frustration with regulations that prioritize long-term system evolution over the users' requests for here-and-now adjustments. Most users accept that go-live inevitably involves uncertainty and extra work, but frustration sets in unless the uncertainty and extra work are short-lived. During continued use, the users expect benefits from the system. They also expect that the implementation team removes barriers to the realization of these benefits.

Many organizational implementations follow a top-down approach that emphasizes the preparations leading up to go-live. This approach leads to expectations of a well-planned implementation with few unanticipated events and an implementation team that takes charge. Other organizational implementations take a bottom-up approach and shift the focus toward design in use. This approach is critically dependent on user participation and mainly suited for systems that can be configured locally, for example by super users. In a study of such an implementation, Hertzum and Torkilsheyggi (2019) find large differences in how the users perceive it. Table 8.1 lists the users' perception of the major pros and cons of the implementation process. The major pros involved the users' appreciation of the gradual realization and incorporation of new possibilities through an engaging process that allowed for meeting local needs in a proactive manner. Probably, the single most important con was the perception that it was a misunderstanding to believe that the users wanted to engage in design in use. This perception was widespread and rooted in experiencing the design-in-use activities as an unwelcome distraction that took time away from the primary work. The users with this perception would have preferred a top-down implementation controlled by the implementation team.

Table 8.1: Users' perception of an organizational implementation that assigned primacy to design in use, based on Hertzum and Torkilsheyggi (2019)

Perceived Pros	Perceived Cons
Design-in-use process gains momentum from early successes and external events	Lack of momentum—especially the implementation of new procedures lags behind
Design in use makes for a proactive and engaging process	A misunderstanding to believe that end-users want to engage in design in use
Design-in-use process allows for meeting local needs	Little local need for the changes that can be accomplished through design in use
Good balance between benefit and the work required to obtain it	Lack of integrations with other systems limits design-in-use possibilities and duplicates work
Gradual realization and incorporation of needs and possibilities	Process has lacked direction, which should have been provided top-down
Design-in-use process provides opportunities for standardization	Lack of standardization restricts the interdepartmental use of the system
Super users are valuable and drive the design-in-use process	Super users lack required knowledge and are not able to drive the implementation process

Table 8.1 shows substantial disagreement in that each of the pros is contested by one of the cons, and vice versa. That is, the users perceive the implementation process in contrasting ways. Relatedly, McGinn et al. (2011) find that nearly all implementation aspects are perceived as barriers by some users and boosters by other users. Super users tend to perceive organizational implementations more positively than other users (Hertzum and Torkilsheyggi, 2019). Either the users who are more positive about the system and implementation process become super users or the super users' larger involvement in the implementation process makes them more positive. The perception of organizational implementations also varies with the user's adopter category (see Section 7.5). Innovators and early adopters embrace new systems and appreciate opportunities to tinker with them. The late majority and laggards are skeptical and need more support, training, and step-by-step instruction to start using a new system.

Reijonen and Heikkilä (2006) find that even after a system has entered operational use, managers often have an invalid picture of how it is perceived by its users. The basis for this finding is that users mainly talk to their peers, rather than their manager, about a new system and how to tackle problems with it (Reijonen and Heikkilä, 2006). Thus, the managers remain unaware of the extent of the users' problems. Markus and Keil (1994) disagree. They hold that middle managers will know that the problems that cause partial adoption are real. Therefore, middle managers are often reluctant to enforce mandatory use if a system merely sees partial use. This disagreement illustrates that organizational implementations often leave middle managers in a difficult situation. They are either insufficiently attentive to their staff's problems or insufficiently assertive in executing instructions from the implementation team.

8.4   COMPETENCES NEEDED LOCALLY IN THE IMPLEMENTATION TEAM

For an organizational implementation to succeed, the implementation team must have the competences and authority to accomplish change in all four components of Figure 2.1: people, tasks, technology, and structure. Handling one component poorly is enough to cause trouble and to delay benefits realization, even if the three other components are handled well. However, diverse competences are needed to make people appreciate the qualities of the new system, to devise effective new procedures for accomplishing tasks, to configure the system for local conditions, and to align the organizational structure with the system. Any one person is unlikely to have this mix of competences; an implementation team must be assembled (Kræmmergaard and Rose, 2002; Metz and Bartley, 2020).

The implementation team should be large enough to cover the needed competences, yet small enough to maintain effective communication among the team members. Unless they communicate effectively, the implementation team will make decisions that are informed by only a subset of its members' competences. To facilitate communication, some organizations co-locate the implementation team during the phases of preparations and go-live (Brown and Vessey, 2001). While the implementation team must cover a diverse mix of competences, it should be kept in mind that it is complemented by additional actors, including a steering committee, external consultants, champions, super users, and tinkerers (Figure 1.1).

It is the responsibility of the implementation team to instill change. To do so, it must align the implementation activities with the mandate it has received from the steering committee. This involves coordinating the activities of the implementation team, consultants, champions, super users, and tinkerers. However, it also involves engaging the organization in the change. That is, it involves coordinating the activities of all the users, who are primarily interested in their daily work and merely take a secondary interest in the implementation of the new system. In total, the implementation team needs competences in the following seven areas (Hertzum and Simonsen, 2019).

- *Managing the project*: competence in shaping, maneuvering, and steering the individual implementation activities and the entire implementation project.

- *Understanding practice*: appreciation and knowledge of the local practices in the organization and how they interrelate in constituting the organization at large.

- *Understanding technology*: knowledge about technological opportunities, familiarity with the new system, and knowhow about how to configure it.

- *Preparing change*: competence in envisioning, specifying, and planning organizational change and the implementation activities necessary to make it happen.

- *Making change*: competence in turning plans into reality by informing the users about the system, prompting them to adopt it, and motivating them to change their practices.

- *Assessing change*: competence in following up on whether pursued effects have been realized and whether emergent opportunities call for renewed implementation activities.

- *Personal traits*: the personal impact that follows from being able to talk knowledgeably and convincingly about how the new system will benefit the organization.

It cannot be taken for granted that these seven competences are available in the organization. External consultants are particularly likely to be required to provide competences in technology and change management. However, the presence—or building—of internal competences is important to the improvisational process of continuing design during use. Many of these continued implementation activities must probably be accomplished without a budget that allows for external consultants.

In staffing the implementation team, you should also consider that the mix of competences needed in the team changes over time (Kræmmergaard and Rose, 2002). The implementation team needs the broadest mix of competences during the preparations. The only competences not important during this phase are those in making and assessing change. Go-live hinges on a narrower mix of competences. The critical competences during go-live are about making change and managing the project. During continued use, competences in understanding practice, understanding technology, and assessing change become increasingly important. At this stage, the implementation process also gets less intense and therefore less dependent on project management.

While the implementation process gets less intense during continued use, this stage is the real challenge (Ali and Miller, 2017): benefits realization is in need of follow-up; productivity may still be below baseline; problems exported from earlier stages have to be resolved; and workarounds reveal new opportunities or call for renewed implementation activities. A specific challenge during continued use is strategy blindness (Arvidsson et al., 2014). It results when the users of a new system merely see it as the replacement of one technology with another and, thus, remain blind to its strategic intent of enabling more efficient ways of working. The reasons for strategy blindness include inadequate competences in informing the users about the pursued change, in following up on effects realization, and—possibly—in understanding the relentless pressure exerted by the primary work. To take this pressure into account, the implementation team must acknowledge the users' practice view on organizational implementation.

References

Aanestad, M., Driveklepp, A.M., Sørli, H., and Hertzum, M. (2017). Participatory continuing design: "Living with" videoconferencing in rehabilitation. In A.M. Kanstrup, A. Bygholm, P. Bertelsen, and C. Nøhr (Eds.), *Participatory Design and Health Information Technology* (pp. 45–59). Amsterdam: IOS Press. DOI: 10.3233/978-1-61499-740-5-45. 73, 76

Aanestad, M. and Jensen, T.B. (2016). Collective mindfulness in post-implementation IS adaptation processes. *Information and Organization*, 26(1-2), 13–27. DOI: 10.1016/j.infoandorg.2016.02.001. 75

Aarts, J. and Berg, M. (2006). Same system, different outcomes: Comparing the implementation of computerized physician order entry in two Dutch hospitals. *Methods of Information in Medicine*, 45(1), 53–61. DOI: 10.1055/s-0038-1634037. 1

Aarts, J., Doorewaard, H., and Berg, M. (2004). Understanding implementation: The case of a computerized physician order entry system in a large Dutch university medical center. *Journal of the American Medical Association*, 11(3), 207–216. DOI: 10.1197/jamia.M1372. 18

Adam, F. and O'Doherty, P. (2004). Do ERP implementations have to be lengthy? Lessons from Irish SMEs. In F. Adam and D. Sammon (Eds.), *The Enterprise Resource Planning Decade: Lessons Learned and Issues for the Future* (pp. 114–137). Hershey, PA: IGI Global. DOI: 10.4018/978-1-59140-188-9.ch007. 37

Ali, M. and Miller, L. (2017). ERP system implementation in large enterprises—A systematic literature review. *Journal of Enterprise Information Management*, 30(4), 666–692. DOI: 10.1108/JEIM-07-2014-0071. 57, 83, 89

Alter, S. (2014). Theory of workarounds. *Communications of the Association for Information Systems*, 34, 1041–1066, article 55. DOI: 10.17705/1CAIS.03455. 72, 78

Amabile, T.M., Barsade, S.G., Mueller, J.S., and Staw, B.M. (2005). Affect and creativity at work. *Administrative Science Quarterly*, 50(3), 367–403. DOI: 10.2189/asqu.2005.50.3.367. 22

Andersen, L.B. (2009). What determines the behaviour and performance of health professionals? Public service motivation, professional norms and/or economic incentives? *International Review of Administrative Sciences*, 75(1), 79–97. DOI: 10.1177/0020852308099507. 45

Argyris, C. and Schön, D.A. (1978). *Organizational Learning: A Theory of Action Perspective*. Reading, MA: Addison-Wesley. 12, 13

Arvidsson, V., Holmström, J., and Lyytinen, K. (2014). Information systems use as a strategy practice: A multi-dimensional view of strategic information system implementation and use. *Journal of Strategic Information Systems*, 23(1), 45–61. DOI: 10.1016/j.jsis.2014.01.004. 25, 26, 36, 57, 89

Arvidsson, V. and Mønsted, T. (2018). Generating innovation potential: How digital entrepreneurs conceal, sequence, anchor, and propagate new technology. *Journal of Strategic Information Systems*, 27(4), 369–383. DOI: 10.1016/j.jsis.2018.10.001. 75, 76

Åsand, H.-R.H. and Mørch, A.I. (2006). Super users and local developers: The organization of end-user development in an accounting company. *Journal of Organizational and End User Computing*, 18(4), 1–21. DOI: 10.4018/joeuc.2006100101. 63

Askedal, K., Flak, L.S., and Aanestad, M. (2019). Five challenges for benefits management in complex digitalisation efforts - and a research agenda to address current shortcomings. *Electronic Journal of e-Government*, 17(2), 64–78. DOI: 10.34190/EJEG.17.2.001. 83

Avgerou, C., Lanzara, F., and Willcocks, L. (Eds.). (2009). *Bricolage, Care and Information Systems: Claudio Ciborra's Legacy in Information Systems Research*. New York: Palgrave Macmillan. 78

Bano, M., Zowghi, D., and da Rimini, F. (2017). User satisfaction and system success: An empirical exploration of user involvement in software development. *Empirical Software Engineering*, 22(5), 2339–2372. DOI: 10.1007/s10664-016-9465-1. 37, 39

Bardach, E. (1977). *The Implementation Game: What Happens after a Bill Becomes a Law*. Cambridge, MA: MIT Press. 28

Beath, C.M. (1991). Supporting the information technology champion. *MIS Quarterly*, 15(3), 355–372. DOI: 10.2307/249647. 47

Beerepoot, I., Koorn, J., van de Weerd, I., van den Hooff, B., Leopold, H., and Reijers, H.A. (2019). Working around health information systems: The role of power. In *ICIS2019: Proceedings of the 40th International Conference on Information Systems* (paper 1361). Atlanta, GA: AIS. https://aisel.aisnet.org/icis2019/behavior_is/behavior_is/2. 72

Bhattacherjee, A., Davis, C., and Hikmet, N. (2013). Physian reactions to healthcare IT: An activity-theoretic analysis. In *HICSS2013: Proceedings of the 46th Hawaii International Conference on System Sciences* (pp. 2545–2554). Washington, DC: IEEE. DOI: 10.1109/HICSS.2013.448. 1

Bhattacherjee, A., Davis, C.J., Connolly, A.J., and Hikmet, N. (2018). User response to mandatory IT use: A coping theory perspective. *European Journal of Information Systems*, 27(4), 395–414. DOI: 10.1057/s41303-017-0047-0. 18

Bider, I. and Jalali, A. (2016). Agile business process development: Why, how and when—Applying Nonaka's theory of knowledge transformation to business process development. *Information Systems and E-Business Management*, 14(4), 693–731. DOI: 10.1007/s10257-014-0256-1. 51

Björgvinsson, E., Ehn, P., and Hillgren, P.-A. (2012). Design things and design thinking: Contemporary participatory design challenges. *Design Issues*, 28(3), 101–116. DOI: 10.1162/DESI_a_00165. 29

Boudreau, M.-C. and Robey, D. (2005). Enacting integrated information technology: A human agency perspective. *Organization Science*, 16(1), 3–18. DOI: 10.1287/orsc.1040.0103. 66, 77

Brehm, L., Heinzl, A., and Markus, M.L. (2001). Tailoring ERP systems: A spectrum of choices and their implications. In *HICSS2001: Proceedings of the 34th Hawaii International Conference on System Sciences* (pp. 1–9). Washington, DC: IEEE Press. DOI: 10.1109/HICSS.2001.927130. 43

Brown, C.V. and Vessey, I. (2001). NIBCO's "big bang". *Communications of the Association for Information Systems*, 5, article 1. DOI: 10.17705/1CAIS.00501. 50, 51, 52, 55, 62, 88

Burke, C.M. and Morley, M.J. (2016). On temporary organizations: A review, synthesis and research agenda. *Human Relations*, 69(6), 1235–1258. DOI: 10.1177/0018726715610809. 76

Button, G. and Sharrock, W. (2009). *Studies of Work and the Workplace in HCI: Concepts and Techniques*. San Rafael, CA: Morgan & Claypool. DOI: 10.2200/S00177ED1V01Y-200903HCI003. 37

By, R.T. (2005). Organisational change management: A critical review. *Journal of Change Management*, 5(4), 369–380. DOI: 10.1080/14697010500359250. 65

Bygstad, B. (2017). Generative innovation: A comparison of lightweight and heavyweight IT. *Journal of Information Technology*, 32(2), 180–193. DOI: 10.1057/jit.2016.15. 15

Carnevale, D. (2003). *Organizational Development in the Public Sector*. Boulder, CO: Westview Press. DOI: 10.4324/9780429498558. 20

Chen, Z., Li, Y., Wu, Y., and Luo, J. (2017). The transition from traditional banking to mobile internet finance: An organizational innovation perspective—A comparative study of Citibank and ICBC. *Financial Innovation*, 3, article 12. DOI: 10.1186/s40854-017-0062-0. 1

Cook, R. and Rasmussen, J. (2005). "Going solid": A model of system dynamics and consequences for patient safety. *BMJ Quality and Safety*, 14(2), 130–134. DOI: 10.1136/qshc.2003.009530. 26

Culp, L.M., Adams, J.A., Byron, J.S., and Boyer, E.A. (2005). Phased implementation. In J.M. Walker, E.J. Bieber, and F. Richards (Eds.), *Implementing an Electronic Health Record System* (pp. 111–119). London: Springer. DOI: 10.1007/1-84628-115-6_14. 51, 53, 55, 63

Daft, R.L. and Lengel, R.H. (1986). Organizational information requirements, media richness and structural design. *Management Science*, 32(5), 554–571. DOI: 10.1287/mnsc.32.5.554. 24

Davis, F.D., Bagozzi, R.P., and Warshaw, P.R. (1989). User acceptance of computer technology: A comparison of two theoretical models. *Management Science*e, 35(8), 982–1003. DOI: 10.1287/mnsc.35.8.982. 20

Davis, F.D., Bagozzi, R.P., and Warshaw, P.R. (1992). Extrinsic and intrinsic motivation to use computers in the workplace. *Journal of Applied Social Psychology*, 22(14), 1111–1132. DOI: 10.1111/j.1559-1816.1992.tb00945.x. 21

DeLone, W.H., and McLean, E.R. (2003). The DeLone and McLean model of information systems success: A ten-year update. *Journal of Management Information Systems*, 19(4), 9–30. DOI: 10.1080/07421222.2003.11045748. 23

Dittrich, Y., Bolmsten, J., and Eriksson, J. (2017). End user development and infrastructuring - Sustaining organizational innovation capabilities. In F. Paternó and V. Wulf (Eds.), *New Perspectives in End-User Development* (pp. 165–206). Cham: Springer. DOI: 10.1007/978-3-319-60291-2_8. 76, 79

Einhorn, F., Marnewick, C., and Meredith, J. (2019). Achieving strategic benefits from business IT projects: The critical importance of using the business case across the entire project lifetime. *International Journal of Project Management*, 37(8), 989–1002. DOI: 10.1016/j.ijproman.2019.09.001. 58, 68, 69

Elbanna, A. (2010). Rethinking IS project boundaries in practice: A multiple-projects perspective. *Journal of Strategic Information Systems*, 19(1), 39–51. DOI: 10.1016/j.jsis.2010.02.005. 74, 75, 78

Ellingsen, G., Monteiro, E., and Munkvold, G. (2007). Standardization of work: Co-constructed practice. *The Information Society*, 23(5), 309–326. DOI: 10.1080/01972240701572723. 44

Feldman, M.S. and Orlikowski, W.J. (2011). Theorizing practice and practicing theory. *Organization Science*, 22(5), 1240–1253. DOI: 10.1287/orsc.1100.0612. 4

Ferneley, E.H. and Sobreperez, P. (2006). Resist, comply or workaound? An examination of different facets of user engagement with information systems. *European Journal of Information Systems*, 15(4), 345–356. DOI: 10.1057/palgrave.ejis.3000629. 72

Fichman, R.G. and Kemerer, C.F. (1999). The illusory diffusion of innovation: An examination of assimilation gaps. *Information Systems Research*, 10(3), 255–275. DOI: 10.1287/isre.10.3.255. 19

Fisher, C.D. (2010). Happiness at work. *International Journal of Management Reviews*, 12(4), 384–412. DOI: 10.1111/j.1468-2370.2009.00270.x. 22

Fitzgerald, M., Kruschwitz, N., Bonnet, D., and Welch, M. (2014). Embracing digital technology: A new strategic imperative. *Sloan Management Review*, 55(2), 1–12. 1, 25, 86

Francoise, O., Bourgault, M., and Pellerin, R. (2009). ERP implementation through critical success factors' management. *Business Process Management Journal*, 15(3), 371–394. DOI: 10.1108/14637150910960620. 62, 69

Gallivan, M.J. (2001). Organizational adoption and assimilation of complex technological innovations: Development and application of a new framework. *The Data Base for Advances in Information Systems*, 32(3), 51–85. DOI: 10.1145/506724.506729. 17, 18

Garside, P. (2004). Are we suffering from change fatigue? *BMJ Quality and Safety*, 13(2), 89–90. DOI: 10.1136/qshc.2003.009159. 25, 27

Gattiker, T.F. and Goodhue, D.L. (2005). What happens after ERP implementation: Understanding the impact of interdependence and differentiation on plant-level outcomes. *MIS Quarterly*, 29(3), 559–585. DOI: 10.2307/25148695. 56

Germonprez, M., Hovorka, D., and Gal, U. (2011). Secondary design: A case of behavioral design science research. *Journal of the Association for Information Systems*, 12(10), 662–683. DOI: 10.17705/1jais.00278. 29, 67, 75

Gerow, J.E., Ayyagari, R., Thatcher, J.B., and Roth, P.L. (2013). Can we have fun @ work? The role of intrinsic motivation for utilitarian systems. *European Journal of Information Systems*, 22(3), 360–380. DOI: 10.1057/ejis.2012.25. 22

Granlien, M.S. and Hertzum, M. (2009). Implementing new ways of working: Interventions and their effect on the use of an electronic medication record. In *Proceedings of the GROUP2009 Conference on Supporting Group Work* (pp. 321–330). New York: ACM Press. DOI: 10.1145/1531674.1531722. 39, 41, 70

Granlien, M.S. and Hertzum, M. (2012). Barriers to the adoption and use of an electronic medication record. *Electronic Journal of Information Systems Evaluation*, 15(2), 216–227. 1, 18

Grudin, J. (1994). Groupware and social dynamics: Eight challenges for developers. *Communications of the ACM*, 37(1), 92-105. DOI: 10.1145/175222.175230. 18, 22

Gupta, S., Bostrom, R.P., and Huber, M. (2010). End-user training methods: What we know, need to know. *The Data Base for Advances in Information Systems*, 41(4), 9–39. DOI: 10.1145/1899639.1899641. 42

Haines, M.N. (2009). Understanding enterprise system customization: An exploration of implementation realities and the key influence factors. *Information Systems Management*, 26(2), 182–198. DOI: 10.1080/10580530902797581. 23, 36, 44, 84

Häkkinen, L. and Hilmola, O.-P. (2008). ERP evaluation during the shakedown phase: Lessons from an after-sales division. *Information Systems Journal*, 18(1), 73–100. DOI: 10.1111/j.1365-2575.2007.00261.x. 60

Halbesleben, J.R.B., Wakefield, D.S., Ward, M.M., Brokel, J., and Crandall, D. (2009). The relationship between super users' attitudes and employee experience with clinical information systems. *Medical Care Research and Review*, 66(1), 82–96. DOI: 10.1177/1077558708325984. 63

Heere, B. (2018). Embracing the sportification of society: Defining e-sports through a polymorphic view on sport. *Sport Management Review*, 21(1), 21–24. DOI: 10.1016/j.smr.2017.07.002. 1

Heikkilä, J., Vahtera, H., and Reijonen, P. (2003). Taking organizational implementation seriously: The case of IOS implementation. In J. Damsgaard and H.Z. Henriksen (Eds.), *Networked Information Technologies: Diffusion and Adoption. Proceedings of the IFIP WG 8.6 International Working Conference on Transfer and Diffusion of IT* (pp. 181–198). Boston, MA: Springer. DOI: 10.1007/1-4020-7862-5_11. 67

Hertzum, M. (2002). Organisational implementation: A complex but under-recognised aspect of information-system design. In *NordiCHI2002: Proceedings of the Second Nordic Conference on Human-Computer Interaction* (pp. 201–204). New York: ACM Press. DOI: 10.1145/572020.572045. 52

Hertzum, M. (2008). On the process of software design: Sources of complexity and reasons for muddling through. In *Proceedings of the EIS2007 Conference on Engineering Interactive Systems* (Vol. LNCS 4940, pp. 483–500). Berlin: Springer. DOI: 10.1007/978-3-540-92698-6_29. 60

Hertzum, M. (2011). Electronic emergency-department whiteboards: A study of clinicians' expectations and experiences. *International Journal of Medical Informatics*, 80(9), 618–630. DOI: 10.1016/j.ijmedinf.2011.06.004. 82

Hertzum, M. (2018). Three contexts for evaluating organizational usability. *Journal of Usability Studies*, 14(1), 35–47. 45

Hertzum, M. (2020). *Usability Testing: A Practitioner's Guide to Evaluating the User Experience*. San Rafael, CA: Morgan & Claypool. DOI: 10.2200/S00987ED1V01Y202001HCI045. 47

Hertzum, M., Bansler, J.P., Havn, E., and Simonsen, J. (2012). Pilot implementation: Learning from field tests in IS development. *Communications of the Association for Information Systems*, 30(1), 313–328. DOI: 10.17705/1CAIS.03020. 45, 46, 47

Hertzum, M. and Ellingsen, G. (2019). The implementation of an electronic health record: Comparing preparations for Epic in Norway with experiences from the UK and Denmark. *International Journal of Medical Informatics*, 129, 312–317. DOI: 10.1016/j.ijmedinf.2019.06.026. 37, 61

Hertzum, M., Manikas, M.I., and Torkilsheyggi, A. (2019). Grappling with the future: The messiness of pilot implementation in information systems design. *Health Informatics Journal*, 25(2), 372–388. DOI: 10.1177/1460458217712058. 47

Hertzum, M. and Simonsen, J. (2011). Effects-driven IT development: Specifying, realizing, and assessing usage effects. *Scandinavian Journal of Information Systems*, 23(1), 3–28. https://aisel.aisnet.org/sjis/vol23/iss1/1. 32, 39, 40, 41, 58, 68, 69

Hertzum, M. and Simonsen, J. (2013). Work-practice changes associated with an electronic emergency department whiteboard. *Health Informatics Journal*, 19(1), 46–60. DOI: 10.1177/1460458212454024. 39, 70, 71

Hertzum, M. and Simonsen, J. (2019). Configuring information systems and work practices for each other: What competences are needed locally? *International Journal of Human-Computer Studies*, 122, 242–255. DOI: 10.1016/j.ijhcs.2018.10.006. 88

Hertzum, M. and Simonsen, J. (2020). How come nothing changed? Reflections on the fasting-time project. In *MIE2020: Proceedings of the 30th Medical Informatics Europe Conference* (pp. 971–975). Amsterdam: IOS Press. DOI: 10.3233/SHTI200306. 25

Hertzum, M., Søes, H., and Frøkjær, E. (1993). Information retrieval systems for professionals: A case study of computer supported legal research. *European Journal of Information Systems*, 2(4), 296–303. DOI: 10.1057/ejis.1993.40. 24, 67

Hertzum, M. and Torkilsheyggi, A. (2019). How do users perceive a design-in-use approach to implementation? A healthcare case. In *Proceedings of the INTERACT2019 Conference on Human-Computer Interaction* (Vol. LNCS 11748, pp. 410–430). Cham: Springer. DOI: 10.1007/978-3-030-29387-1_23. 5, 67, 68, 67

Herzberg, F., Mausner, B., and Snyderman, B.B. (1959). *The Motivation to Work*. New York: Wiley. 25

Holt, C. and Laury, S. (2002). Risk aversion and incentive effects. *American Economic Review*, 92(5), 1644–1655. DOI: 10.1257/000282802762024700. 26

Hornbæk, K. and Hertzum, M. (2017). Technology acceptance and user experience: A review of the experiential component in HCI. *ACM Transactions on Computer-Human Interaction*, 24(5), article 33. DOI: 10.1145/3127358. 21

Howard, M.C. and Rose, J.C. (2019). Refining and extending task-technology fit theory: Creation of two task-technology fit scales and empirical clarification of the construct. *Information and Management*, 56(6), article 103134. DOI: 10.1016/j.im.2018.12.002. 3

Inanc-Demir, M. and Kozak, M. (2019). Big data and its supporting elements: Implications for tourism and hospitality marketing. In M. Sigala, R. Rahimi, and M. Thelwall (Eds.), *Big Data and Innovation in Tourism, Travel, and Hospitality: Managerial Approaches, Techniques, and Applications* (pp. 213–223). Singapore: Springer Nature. DOI: 10.1007/978-981-13-6339-9_13. 1

Irani, Z. (2010). Investment evaluation within project management: An information systems perspective. *Journal of the Operational Research Society*, 61(6), 917–928. DOI: 10.1057/jors.2010.10. 68, 69

Isaacson, W. (2011). *Steve Jobs*. New York: Simon and Schuster. 83

Janssen, M., van Veenstra, A.F., and van der Voort, H. (2013). Management and failure of large transformation projects: Factors affecting user adoption. In Y.K. Dwivedi, H.Z. Henriksen, D. Wastell, and R. De' (Eds.), *Grand Successes and Failures in IT: Public and Private Sectors. Proceedings of the IFIP WG 8.6 International Working Conference on Transfer and Diffusion of IT* (pp. 121–135). Heidelberg: Springer. DOI: 10.1007/978-3-642-38862-0_8. 36, 39

Jeyaraj, A. and Sabherwal, R. (2008). Adoption of information systems innovation by individuals: A study of processes involving contextual, adopter, and influencer actions. *Information and Organization*, 18(3), 205–234. DOI: 10.1016/j.infoandorg.2008.04.001. 19

Johannessen, L.K. and Ellingsen, G. (2009). Integration and generification - Agile software development in the healthcare market. *Computer Supported Cooperative Work*, 18(5–6), 607-634. DOI: 10.1007/s10606-009-9097-8. 84

Jurison, J. (1996). The temporal nature of IS benefits: A longitudinal study. *Information and Management*, 30(2), 75–79. DOI: 10.1016/0378-7206(95)00050-X. 57

Karasti, H., Baker, K., and Millerand, F. (2010). Infrastructure time: Long-term matters in collaborative development. *Computer Supported Cooperative Work*, 19(3&4), 377–415. DOI: 10.1007/s10606-010-9113-z. 5, 67, 82

Keen, P.G.W. (1981). Information systems and organizational change. *Communications of the ACM*, 24(1), 24–33. DOI: 10.1145/358527.358543. 25, 27, 28

King, W.R. and He, J. (2006). A meta-analysis of the technology acceptance model. *Information and Management*, 43(6), 740–755. DOI: 10.1016/j.im.2006.05.003. 20

Ko, A.J., Abraham, R., Beckwith, L., Blackwell, A., Burnett, M., Erwig, M., et al. (2011). The state of the art in end-user software engineering. *ACM Computing Surveys*, 43(3), article 21. DOI: 10.1145/1922649.1922658. 76

Kotter, J.P. (2008). *A Sense of Urgency*. Boston, MA: Harvard Business Press. 25

Kræmmergaard, P. and Rose, J. (2002). Managerial competences for ERP journeys. *Information Systems Frontiers*, 4(2), 199–211. DOI: 10.1023/A:1016054904008. 30, 88, 89

Kujala, S. and Kauppinen, M. (2004). Identifying and selecting users for user-centered design. In *NordiCHI2004: Proceedings of the Third Nordic Conference on Human-Computer Interaction* (pp. 297–303). New York: ACM Press. DOI: 10.1145/1028014.1028060. 37

Kwahk, K.-Y. and Ahn, H. (2010). Moderating effects of localization differences on ERP use: A socio-technical systems perspective. *Computers in Human Behavior*, 26(2), 186–198. DOI: 10.1016/j.chb.2009.10.006. 36

Lavie, D., Stettner, U., and Tushman, M.L. (2010). Exploration and exploitation within and across organizations. *Academy of Management Annals*, 4(1), 109–155. DOI: 10.1080/19416521003691287. 78

Leavitt, H.J. (1965). Applied organizational change in industry: Structural, technological and humanistic approaches. In J.G. March (Ed.), *Handbook of Organizations* (pp. 1144–1170). London: Routledge. DOI: 10.4324/9780203629130. 9, 10

Leon, A. (2019). *Enterprise Resource Planning*. Fourth edition. New Delhi: McGraw-Hill. 51

Leonard-Barton, D. (1988). Implementation as mutual adaptation of technology and organization. *Research Policy*, 17(5), 251–267. DOI: 10.1016/0048-7333(88)90006-6. 1

Leonardi, P.M. (2009). Crossing the implementation line: The mutual constitution of technology and organizing across development and use activities. *Communication Theory*, 19(3), 278–310. DOI: 10.1111/j.1468-2885.2009.01344.x. 32

Leorke, D., Wyatt, D., and McQuire, S. (2018). "More than just a library": Public libraries in the 'smart city'. *City, Culture and Society*, 15, 37–44. DOI: 10.1016/j.ccs.2018.05.002. 1

Longhurst, C.A., Davis, T., Maneker, A., Eschenroeder, H.C., Dunscombe, R., Reynolds, G., et al. (2019). Local investment in training drives electronic health record user satisfaction. *Appied Clinical Informatics*, 10(2), 331–335. DOI: 10.1055/s-0039-1688753. 44

Maas, J.-B., van Fenema, P.C., and Soeters, J. (2014). ERP system usage: The role of control and empowerment. *New Technology, Work and Employment*, 29(1), 88–103. DOI: 10.1111/ntwe.12021. 36, 68, 79

Maas, J.-B., van Fenema, P.C., and Soeters, J. (2016). ERP as an organizational innovation: Key users and cross-boundary knowledge management. *Journal of Knowledge Management*, 20(3), 557–577. DOI: 10.1108/JKM-05-2015-0195. 74, 76, 77

Malaurent, J. and Avison, D. (2016). Reconciling global and local needs: A canonical action research project to deal with workarounds. *Information Systems Journal*, 26(3), 227–257. DOI: 10.1111/isj.12074. 36

Markus, M.L. (2004). Technochange management: Using IT to drive organizational change. *Journal of Information Technology*, 19(1), 4–20. DOI: 10.1057/palgrave.jit.2000002. 1, 3, 58, 74

Markus, M.L. and Keil, M. (1994). If we built it, they will come: Designing information systems that people want to use. *Sloan Management Review*, 35(4), 11–25. 32, 45, 87

Markus, M.L. and Mao, J.-Y. (2004). Participation in development and implementation - Updating an old, tired concept for today's IS contexts. *Journal of the Association for Information Systems*, 5(11–12), 514-544. DOI: 10.17705/1jais.00057. 24, 37

McAfee, A. (2002). The impact of enterprise information technology adoption on operational performance: An empirical investigation. *Production and Operations Management*, 11(1), 33–53. DOI: 10.1111/j.1937-5956.2002.tb00183.x. 50, 56, 57

McGinn, C.A., Grenier, S., Duplantie, J., Shaw, N., Sicotte, C., Mathieu, L., Leduc, Y., Lágare, F., and Gagnon, M.-P. (2011). Comparison of user groups' perspectives of barriers and facilitators to implementing electronic health records: A systematic review. *BMC Medicine*, 9, article 46. DOI: 10.1186/1741-7015-9-46. 36, 57, 87

McMillan, K. and Perron, A. (2013). Nurses amidst change: The concept of change fatigue offers an alternative perspective on organizational change. *Policy, Politics, and Nursing Practice*, 14(1), 26–32. DOI: 10.1177/1527154413481811. 27

Metz, A. and Bartley, L. (2020). Implementation teams: A stakeholder view of leading and sustaining change. In B. Albers, A. Shlonsky, and R. Mildon (Eds.), *Implementation Science 3.0* (pp. 199–225). Cham: Springer. DOI: 10.1007/978-3-030-03874-8_8. 2, 88

Miettinen, R., Samra-Fredericks, D., and Yanow, D. (2009). Re-turn to practice: An introductory essay. *Organization Studies*, 30(12), 1309–1327. DOI: 10.1177/0170840609349860. 4

Mintzberg, H. (1980). Structure in 5's: A synthesis of the research on organization design. *Management Science*, 26(3), 322–341. DOI: 10.1287/mnsc.26.3.322. 14

Mønsted, T., Hertzum, M., and Søndergaard, J. (2020). A socio-temporal perspective on pilot implementation: Bootstrappng preventive care. *Computer Supported Cooperative Work*, 29(4), 419–449. DOI: 10.1007/s10606-019-09369-6. 46, 47

Montealegre, R. and Keil, M. (2000). De-escalating information technology projects: Lessons from the Denver International Airport. *MIS Quarterly*, 24(3), 417–447. DOI: 10.2307/3250968. 45

Monteiro, E., Pollock, N., Hanseth, O., and Williams, R. (2013). From artefacts to infrastructures. *Computer Supported Cooperative Work*, 22(4-6), 575–607. DOI: 10.1007/s10606-012-9167-1. 81

Moon, M.C., Hills, R., and Demiris, G. (2018). Understanding optimisation processes of electronic health records (EHRs) in select leading hospitals: A qualitative study. *Journal of Innovation in Health Informatics*, 25(2), 109–125. DOI: 10.14236/jhi.v25i2.1011. 65

Mosweu, T.L. and Mosweu, O. (2018). Electronic court records management systems: A review of literature in selected African countries. *Mousaion*, 36(4), 1–21. DOI: /10.25159/2663-659X/4196. 1

Müller, S.D., Mathiassen, L., Saunders, C.S., and Kræmmergaard, P. (2017). Political maneuvering during business process transformation: A pluralist approach. *Journal of the Association for Information Systems*, 18(3), 173–205. DOI: 10.17705/1jais.00454. 25, 28

Mumford, E. (1983). *Designing Human Systems for New Technology: The Ethics Method*. Manchester, UK: Manchester Business School. 37Nilsen, P., Schildmeijer, K., Ericsson, C., Seing, I., and Birken, S. (2019). Implementation of change in health care in Sweden: A qualitative study of professionals' change responses. *Implementation Science*, 14, article 51. DOI: 10.1186/s13012-019-0902-6. 28

Norton, A.L., Coulson-Thomas, Y.M., Coulson-Thomas, C.J., and Ashurst, C. (2012). Delivering training for highly demanding information systems. *European Journal of Training and Development*, 36(6), 646–662. DOI: 10.1108/03090591211245530. 42, 48, 77

Nworie, J. and Haughton, N. (2008). Good intentions and unanticipated effects: The unintended consequences of the application of technology in teaching and learning environments. *TechTrends*, 52(5), 52–58. DOI: 10.1007/s11528-008-0197-y. 54

Obwegeser, N., Danielsen, P., Hansen, K.S., Helt, M.A., and Nielsen, L.H. (2019). Selection and training of super-users for ERP implementation projects. *Journal of Information Technology Case and Application Research*, 21(2), 74–89. DOI: 10.1080/15228053.2019.1631606. 61, 62, 77

Olson, J.S. and Olson, G.M. (2014). *Working Together Apart: Collaboration over the Internet*. San Rafael, CA: Morgan & Claypool. DOI: 10.2200/S00542ED1V01Y201310HCI020. 1, 44

Orlikowski, W.J. (1996). Improvising organizational transformation over time: A situated change perspective. *Information Systems Research*, 7(1), 63–92. DOI: 10.1287/isre.7.1.63. 4, 12, 78

Orlikowski, W.J. (2000). Using technology and constituting structures: A practice lens for studying technology in organizations. *Organization Science*, 11(4), 404–428. DOI: 10.1287/orsc.11.4.404.14600. 26, 44

Owens, K. (2008). EMR implementation: Big bang or phased approach? *Journal of Medical Practice Management*, 23(5), 279–281. 50, 51, 52, 55

Pal, R., Sengupta, A., and Bose, I. (2008). Role of pilot study in assessing viability of new technology projects: The case of RFID in parking operations. *Communications of the Association for Information Systems*, 23, 257–276, article 15. DOI: 10.17705/1CAIS.02315. 47

Pan, M.-Z. and Mao, J.-Y. (2016). Cross boundary mechanisms for knowledge management by user representatives in enterprise systems implementation. *IEEE Transactions on Engineering Management*, 63(4), 438–450. DOI: 10.1109/TEM.2016.2596319. 63

Parks, R., Xu, H., Chu, C.-H., and Lowry, P.B. (2017). Examining the intended and unintended consequences of organisational privacy safeguards. *European Journal of Information Systems*, 26(1), 37–65. DOI: 10.1057/s41303-016-0001-6. 54

Pearce, J., Mann, M.K., Jones, C., van Buschbach, S., Olff, M., and Bisson, J.I. (2012). The most effective way of delivering a train-the-trainers program: A systematic review. *Journal of Continuing Education in the Health Professions*, 32(3), 215–226. DOI: 10.1002/chp.21148. 42

Petter, S., DeLone, W., and McLean, E.R. (2013). Information systems success: The quest for the independent variables. *Journal of Management Information Systems*, 29(4), 7–61. DOI: 10.2753/MIS0742-1222290401. 18, 21, 22, 23

Pollock, N., Williams, R., and D'Adderio, L. (2007). Global software and its provenance: Generification work in the production of organizational software packages. *Social Studies of Science*, 37(2), 254–280. DOI: 10.1177/0306312706066022. 84

Powell, S.G., Baker, K.R., and Lawson, B. (2008). A critical review of the literature on spreadsheet errors. *Decision Support Systems*, 46(1), 128–138. DOI: 10.1016/j.dss.2008.06.001. 76

Pries-Heje, L. and Dittrich, Y. (2009). ERP implementation as design: Looking at participatory design for means to facilitate knowledge integration. *Scandinavian Journal of Information Systems*, 21(2), 27–58. https://aisel.aisnet.org/sjis/vol21/iss2/4. 10, 11

Rasmussen, R., Christensen, A.S., Fjeldsted, T., and Hertzum, M. (2011). Selecting users for participation in IT projects: Trading a representative sample for advocates and champions? *Interacting with Computers*, 23(2), 176–187. DOI: 10.1016/j.intcom.2011.02.006. 21, 30, 37, 38

Rasmussen, R., Fleron, B., Hertzum, M., and Simonsen, J. (2010). Balancing tradition and transcendence in the implementation of emergency-department electronic whiteboards. In J. Molka-Danielsen, H.W. Nicolaisen, and J.S. Persson (Eds.), *Selected Papers of the Information Systems Research Seminar in Scandinavia 2010* (pp. 73–87). Trondheim, NO: Tapir Academic Press. 82

Reich, B.H. and Benbasat, I. (2000). Factors that influence the social dimension of alignment between business and information technology objectives. *MIS Quarterly*, 24(1), 81–113. DOI: 10.2307/3250980. 65

Reijonen, P. and Heikkilä, J. (2006). The planned and materialized implementation of an information system. In M. Khosrowpour (Ed.), *Cases on Strategic Information Systems* (pp. 116–130). Hershey, PA: IGI Global. DOI: 10.4018/978-1-59904-414-9.ch008. 60, 63, 87

Ribes, D. and Finholt, T.A. (2009). The long now of technology infrastructure: Articulating tensions in development. *Journal of the Association for Information Systems*, 10(5), 375–398. DOI: 10.17705/1jais.00199. 67

Rogers, E.M. (2003). *Diffusion of Innovations*. Fifth edition. New York: Free Press. 47, 48, 78, 79

Rohde, M. and Wulf, V. (2018). Integrated organization and technology development (OTD): A critical evaluation. In V. Wulf, V. Pipek, D. Randall, M. Rohde, K. Schmidt, and G. Stevens (Eds.), *Socio-Informatics: A Practice-Based Perspective on the Design and Use of IT Artefacts* (pp. 279–302). Oxford: Oxford University Press. DOI: 10.1093/oso/9780198733249.003.0009. 14, 32, 83

Rolland, K.H. and Monteiro, E. (2002). Balancing the local and the global in infrastructural information systems. *The Information Society*, 18(2), 87–100. DOI: 10.1080/01972240290075020. 36

Ross, J.W. (1999). Surprising facts about implementing ERP. *IT Professional*, 1(4), 65–68. DOI: 10.1109/6294.781626. 52, 56, 57, 66

Ryan, R.M. and Deci, E.L. (2000). Intrinsic and extrinsic motivations: Classic definitions and new directions. *Contemporary Educational Psychology*, 25(1), 54–67. DOI: 10.1006/ceps.1999.1020. 24

Sabherwal, R., Jeyaraj, A., and Chowa, C. (2006). Information system success: Individual and organizational determinants. *Management Science*, 52(12), 1849–1864. DOI: 10.1287/mnsc.1060.0583. 18, 42

Saeed, K.A., Abdinnour, S., Lengnick-Hall, M.L., and Lengnick-Hall, C.A. (2010). Examining the impact of pre-implementation expectations on post-implementation use of enterprise systems: A longitudinal study. *Decision Sciences*, 41(4), 659–688. DOI: 10.1111/j.1540-5915.2010.00285.x. 57

Safadi, H. and Faraj, S. (2010). The role of workarounds during an open source electronic medical record system implementation. In *ICIS2010: Proceedings of the International Conference on Information Systems* (paper 47). Atlanta, GA: AIS. https://aisel.aisnet.org/icis2010_submissions/47. 74

Santamaría-Sánchez, L., Núñez-Nickel, M., and Gago-Rodríguez, S. (2010). The role played by interdependences in ERP implementations: An empirical analysis of critical factors that minimize elapsed time. *Information and Management*, 47(2), 87–95. DOI: 10.1016/j.im.2009.10.004. 37, 44

Sarkis, J. and Sundaray, R.P. (2003). Managing large-scale global enterprise resource planning systems: A case study at Texas Instruments. *International Journal of Information Management*, 23(5), 431–442. DOI: 10.1016/S0268-4012(03)00070-7. 51, 52

Schneider, C. and Sarker, S. (2006). A case of information systems pre-implementation failure: Pitfalls of overlooking the key stakeholders' interests. In M. Khosrowpour (Ed.), *Cases on Strategic Information Systems* (pp. 32–48). Hershey, PA: IGI Global. DOI: 10.4018/978-1-59904-414-9.ch003. 38

Schön, D.A. (1963). Champions for radical new inventions. *Harvard Business Review*, 41(2), 77–86. 48

Scott, J.E. and Vessey, I. (2000). Implementing enterprise resource planning systems: The role of learning from failure. *Information Systems Frontiers*, 2(2), 213–232. DOI: 10.1023/A:1026504325010. 27

Sedera, D. and Lokuge, S. (2020). Does it get better over time? A longitudinal assessment of enterprise system user performance. *Information Technology and People*, 33(4), 1098–1123. DOI: 10.1108/ITP-01-2019-0005. 57

Sergeeva, A., Aij, K., van den Hoof, B., and Huysman, M. (2016). Mobile devices in the operating room: Intended and unintended consequences for nurses' work. *Health Informatics Journal*, 22(4), 1101–1110. DOI: 10.1177/1460458215598637. 54

Shao, Z., Feng, Y., and Hu, Q. (2016). Effectiveness of top management support in enterprise systems success: A contingency perspective of fit between leadership style and system life-cycle. *European Journal of Information Systems*, 25(2), 131–153. DOI: 10.1057/ejis.2015.6. 18

Sharma, R. and Yetton, P. (2007). The contingent effects of training, technical complexity, and task interdependence on successful information systems implementation. *MIS Quarterly*, 31(2), 219–238. DOI: 10.2307/25148789. 42

Shaul, L. and Tauber, D. (2013). Critical success factors in enterprise resource planning systems: Review of the last decade. *ACM Computing Surveys*, 45(4), article 55. DOI: 10.1145/2501654.2501669. 29

Simon, H.A. (1996). *The Sciences of the Artificial.* Third edition. Cambridge, MA: MIT Press. 29

Simonsen, J. and Hertzum, M. (2012). Sustained participatory design: Extending the iterative approach. *Design Issues*, 28(3), 10–21. DOI: 10.1162/DESI_a_00158. 69

Simonsen, J., Hertzum, M., and Barlach, A. (2011). Experiences with effects specifications. In M. Hertzum and C. Jørgensen (Eds.), *Balancing Sourcing and Innovation in Information Systems Development* (pp. 145–163). Trondheim, NO: Tapir Academic Press. 41

Simonsen, J., Karasti, H., and Hertzum, M. (2020). Infrastructuring and participatory design: Exploring infrastructural inversion as analytic, empirical, and generative. *Computer Supported Cooperative Work*, 29(1-2), 115–151. DOI: 10.1007/s10606-019-09365-w. 40

Soliman, W. and Rinta-Kahila, T. (2020). Toward a refined conceptualization of IS discontinuance: Reflection on the past and a way forward. *Information and Management*, 57(2), article 103167. DOI: 10.1016/j.im.2019.05.002. 19

Spencer, M. (2015). Brittleness and bureaucracy: Software as a material for science. *Perspectives on Science*, 23(4), 466–484. DOI: 10.1162/POSC_a_00184. 86

Standish Group. (2020). *CHAOS Report: Beyond Infinity.* Boston, MA: The Standish Group. 1, 86

Star, S.L. and Ruhleder, K. (1996). Steps toward an ecology of infrastructure: Design and access for large information spaces. *Information Systems Research*, 7(1), 111–134. DOI: 10.1287/isre.7.1.111. 82

Suchman, L.A. (2007). *Human-Machine Reconfigurations: Plans and Situated Action.* 2nd edition. Cambridge, UK: Cambridge University Press. 36

Tam, K.Y., Feng, Y., and Lai, M.C. (2019). Effective use of policing systems: A two-stage study of the shakedown period of system implementation. *IEEE Transactions on Engineering Management*. DOI: 10.1109/TEM.2019.2938983. 57

Thakhathi, A. (2018). Champions of change and organizational development: A return to Schön and typology for future research and practice. In D.A. Noumair and A.B. Shani (Eds.), *Research in Organizational Change and Development* (Vol. 26, pp. 265–306). Somerville, MA: Emerald. DOI: 10.1108/S0897-301620180000026007. 47

Torkilsheyggi, A. and Hertzum, M. (2017). Incomplete by design: A study of a design-in-use approach to systems implementation. *Scandinavian Journal of Information Systems*, 29(2), article 2. https://aisel.aisnet.org/sjis/vol29/iss2/2. 60, 76, 82, 86

Tyre, M.J. and Orlikowski, W.J. (1994). Windows of opportunity: Temporal patterns of technological adaptation in organizations. *Organization Science*, 5(1), 98–118. DOI: 10.1287/orsc.5.1.98. 26, 50, 60

Uppström, E., Lönn, C.-M., Hoffsten, M., and Thorström, J. (2015). New implications for customization of ERP systems. *In HICSS2015: Proceedings of the 48th Hawaii International Conference on System Sciences* (pp. 4220–4229). Washington, DC: IEEE Press. DOI: 10.1109/HICSS.2015.505. 43

Venkatesh, V. and Davis, F.D. (2000). A theoretical extension of the technology acceptance model: Four longitudinal field studies. *Management Science*, 46(2), 186–204. DOI: 10.1287/mnsc.46.2.186.11926. 20, 21

Venkatesh, V., Morris, M.G., Davis, G.B., and Davis, F.D. (2003). User acceptance of information technology: Toward a unified view. *MIS Quarterly*, 27(3), 425–478. DOI: 10.2307/30036540. 20, 21

Vogelsmeier, A.A., Halbesleben, J.R.B., and Scott-Cawiezell, J.R. (2008). Technology implementation and workarounds in the nursing home. *Journal of the American Medical Informatics Association*, 15(1), 114–119. DOI: 10.1197/jamia.M2378. 77

von Hippel, E. (1986). Lead users: A source of novel product concepts. *Management Science*, 32(7), 791–805. DOI: 10.1287/mnsc.32.7.791. 79

Wagner, E.L. and Newell, S. (2007). Exploring the importance of participation in the post-implementation period of an ES project: A neglected area. *Journal of the Association for Information Systems*, 8(10), 508–524. DOI: 10.17705/1jais.00142. 65, 66, 67

Wagner, E.L. and Piccoli, G. (2007). Moving beyond user participation to achieve successful IS design. *Communications of the ACM*, 50(12), 51–55. DOI: 10.1145/1323688.1323694. 58

Ward, J. and Daniel, E. (2012). *Benefits Management: How to Increase the Business Value of Your IT Projects*, 2nd edition. Chichester, UK: Wiley. 36, 39, 71

Wei, C.-C. (2008). Evaluating the performance of an ERP system based on the knowledge of ERP implementation objectives. *International Journal of Advanced Manufacturing Technology*, 39(1-2), 168–181. DOI: 10.1007/s00170-007-1189-3. 69, 71

Weick, K.E. and Quinn, R.E. (1999). Organizational change and development. *Annual Review of Psychology*, 50, 361–386. DOI: 10.1146/annurev.psych.50.1.361. 11, 12

White, D. and Fortune, J. (2002). Current practice in project management—An empirical study. *International Journal of Project Management*, 20(1), 1–11. DOI: 10.1016/S0263-7863(00)00029-6. 75

Yeung, A.S., Taylor, P.G., Hui, C., Lam-Chiang, A.C., and Low, E.-L. (2012). Mandatory use of technology in teaching: Who cares and so what? *British Journal of Educational Technology*, 43(6), 859–870. DOI: 10.1111/j.1467-8535.2011.01253.x. 18

Yuan, C.T., Bradley, E.H., and Nembhard, I.M. (2015). A mixed methods study of how clinician 'super users' influence others during the implementation of electronic health records. *BMC Medical Informatics and Decision Making*, 15, article 26. DOI: 10.1186/s12911-015-0154-6. 62

Zigurs, I. and Buckland, B.K. (1998). A theory of task/technology fit and group support systems effectiveness. *MIS Quarterly*, 22(3), 313–334. DOI: 10.2307/249668. 3

Author Biography

Morten Hertzum is Professor of Information Science in the Department of Communication at the University of Copenhagen, Denmark. He has a Ph.D. in Computer Science and has previously held positions at Roskilde University, University of Strathclyde, Risø National Laboratory, and University of Limerick. Hertzum has published extensively about the implementation and evaluation of information systems, especially in healthcare organizations. He is also the author of a book on usability testing (published by Morgan & Claypool, 2020). His research interests include human-computer interaction, computer-supported cooperative work, healthcare informatics, and organizational implementation.